two WORLDS one CHANCE

MOSAICA PRESS

TheShmuz *on life*

two
WORLDS
one # CHANCE

RABBI BEN TZION SHAFIER

Mosaica Press, Inc.
© 2018 by Bentzion Shafier
Designed and typeset by Brocha Mirel Strizower

ISBN-10: 1-946351-40-7
ISBN-13: 978-1-946351-40-1

Published by:
Mosaica Press, Inc.
www.mosaicapress.com
info@mosaicapress.com

TO MY MOTHER,

MRS. ISABEL SHAFIER, A"H

ALL THAT I AM, ALL THAT I WILL EVER BE,
IS BECAUSE OF YOU.

Haskamahs for previous *Shmuz* books

Talmudical Institute of Upstate New York

Rabbi Menachem Davidowitz, Dean
Rabbi Daniel Goldstein, Principal

OFFICERS
Rabbi Menachem Davidowitz
  President
Rabbi Shlomo Noble
  Executive VP
Michael Roth
  Treasurer
Gerald I. Segelman
  Secretary

FOUNDERS
Arnold Becker
Jack Binik
Nathan Carr
Morris Davidowitz
Morris Diamond
Abraham Feldman
Milton Fisher
S. Glick
Irving Gordon
Louis Gross
Samuel Harris
Aaron Heimowitz
Hyman Kolko
Benjamin Krieger
Barnet Levy
Leo Lisker
Hyman Mandell
Frederick Margareten
J. Bernard Merzel
Sol Merzel
William Merzel
Jerome Miller
Seymour Morris
Sydney Morris
Jack Newhouse
Goodwin Nusbaum
Harris Nusbaum
Howard I. Nusbaum
Benjamin Robfogel
Maurice M. Rothman
Irwin S. Schulman
Donald Schwartz
Soloman Schwartz
Ernest Tamary
Zev Wolfson

DIVISIONS
HIGH SCHOOL
  מתיבתא ידרן שה
  Maurice M. Rothman
BAIS MEDRASH
KOLLEL
ADULT EDUCATION
  Anshei Kipel Velin
K-8 SCHOOL
  Derrech HaTorah

September 20, 2010

This sefer is a powerful and dramatic presentation of the foundations of our faith.

It is written for the 21st century reader with all of the wisdom and color of the Shmuz on the Parsha.

May the Rebono Shel Olam help Rabbi Shafier to be able to continue to spread the D'var Hashem.

With Torah Greetings,

Rabbi Menachem Davidowitz

769 Park Avenue Rochester, New York 14607 Phone (585) 473-2810 Fax (585) 442-0417

בס"ד

שמואל קמנצקי
Rabbi S. Kamenetsky

2018 Upland Way
Philadelphia, PA 19131

Home: 215-473-2798
Study: 215-473-1212

October 5, 2010

Rabbi Ben Tzion Shafier
10 Mariner Way
Monsey, NY 10952

Dear Rabbi Shafier, שליט"א

Thank you for sending your manuscript, the "Shmuz on Life - Stop Surviving and Start Living." It is enjoyable reading and clearly and easily understandable. May it benefit the entire כלל ישראל.

My sincere ברכה to you is that your forthcoming book will fulfill your wish to help אחינו בני ישראל find true meaning and happiness in their lives.

May you be blessed with הצלחה in all your endeavors.

S. Kamenetsky

Rabbi CHAIM P. SCHEINBERG
Rosh Hayeshiva "TORAH ORE"
and Morah Hora'ah of Kiryat Mattersdorf

חרב חיים פינחם שיינברג
ראש ישיבת 'תורה אור'
ומורה הוראה דקרית ממרסדורף

כבוד ידידי מאד הרב הגה"ח הרב נשא"ה גדול בכ' נ/צ/ון בעיר ואם...
לפני הראש... הבא/מרה מנקד/רני של תורה/ראינו שלא
ובכן רחמ... ובעורי בנקד/ראור דבר מוסר וגמ/חורות
מ/ם/ם/ה כרך גם ון א/ הכיר הבל/ן מ/פ/גל שרא
כאשר הו רמל.. פ/ם/צוהן ם/ם/ר היט וגגן/י/ער/ך
דגורה וגו/ם/ם/ם/ם/ר... אחת ולצו... אישוגן/ולם...
בזאת ...

ולג/ שמם ב/ם/ם/ר/... אלל/ אלל
חוט/ן ורח/ם/ן הם/ם/ם/ם/ר...
המדבר ראה שלא...

חיים פינחס

TABLE OF CONTENTS

One: Introduction: What Am I Doing Here? 1

Two: David 4

Three: Appreciating Our Wealth. 8

Four: Of Course I'm Happy. Aren't I? 17

Five: The Voice Inside 29

Six: Loving Life and Killing Time 43

Seven: God Blew It 49

Eight: What Am I Doing Here? 58

Nine: Who Are You? 61

Ten: The Purpose of It All. 67

Eleven: "I" Am Not My Body 70

Twelve: Pleasure Without a Body. 75

Thirteen: Hello, This Is My Funeral 80

Fourteen: WYSIWYG: What You See Is What You Get 83

Fifteen: Actors on the Stage 90

Sixteen: Animal Soul/Spiritual Soul 100

Seventeen: The Pants-Too-Short Syndrome 111

Eighteen: Torah from Sinai 120

Nineteen: People Believe What They Want to Believe 133

Twenty: I Never Do Anything Wrong. 149

Twenty-One: I'll Never Die 162

Twenty-Two: Frank and Joe 176

Twenty-Three: The Eternal People. 183

Conclusion. 200

Afterword 202

Chapter One

INTRODUCTION: WHAT AM I DOING HERE?

If you don't know where you are going,
it doesn't matter which road you take!

(The Cheshire Cat, *Alice in Wonderland*)

L ittle children are so curious. They are always asking *why this* and *why that*. Why is the sky blue, and why do ducks have webbed feet? Why is there sand on the beach? Why does a ball fall down and not up? Why, why, why?

Isn't it sad that when we grow up, we stop asking questions? It isn't so much that we know all of the answers. It's more that we lose hope of finding real answers. During our school years we are trained to accept things: *That's the way it is. That's the way it's always been. Just accept it.*

After a while, we realize that these are the types of answers that the people around us are happy with, and we start questioning less and less, until we lose the ability to even question at all. We even stop asking those questions that lead to the pat answers — we become socialized into acceptance. *That's the way it is. That's the way it's always been. Just do it, and stop asking so many questions. We don't need questions around here; we need people who get things done!*

It's unfortunate that we lose that instinctive desire to know why, because from questions come knowledge, and from knowledge comes understanding.

However, the one "why" that a thinking, intelligent human being can *never* stop asking is: Why am I here? I accept that Hashem created the world. I know that Hashem created the galaxies, the cosmos, and all that they contain. I also understand that Hashem created me — but why? What is my purpose? Why am I alive? *Why did Hashem make me?*

We human beings are a curious breed. We go about life, busy as beavers, with plans and goals — five-year goals, ten-year goals. I will live here. Get that job. Marry that sort of person. Send my children to that sort of school. Teach them these life lessons. We have it all worked out, all well-planned. Yet we might not have the foundation to it all. Why do it? Why pursue it? What is the purpose of it all?

Can I live without knowing the answer to this question? Isn't this the most fundamental question that a human *must* answer? Forget philosophy, forget religion; there is one simple, vital question that demands an answer: **What am I doing here?** Why did God create me? What is my purpose in life?

How can I get up in the morning and pursue a life course without an answer to this question? How can I raise a family? What do I teach my children? This question frames everything we do, everything we value, and everything we impart as life lessons to those we love. If I am alive, if I am a thinking, intelligent person, how can I continue without a solid answer to this most elementary question: **What is the purpose of my life?**

Chapter Two

DAVID

It was a Tuesday afternoon, and I was sitting in my study when the phone rang. It was a voice I hadn't heard in quite a while.

"Hi, Rabbi, this is David Goldstein. Do you remember me? I was in your Sunday morning class on Judaism a while ago."

It took me a moment to place the name — it *had* been quite some time. "Of course I remember you, David. How are you? What are you up to these days?"

There was a certain urgency in his voice when he said, "Well, Rabbi, that's the thing. I need to talk to you. Is there a time I can come by?"

"Sure, I'd love to see you," I said. "How about this afternoon? If that works for you, come on by."

It was a good thing he had called before stopping by, because I never would have recognized him. In my mind, he was still sixteen years old, wearing tattered jeans with rumpled hair. I remembered him as he was back in our Sunday morning class: a bright, inquisitive young man, so full of life, with an impetuous vibrancy that was contagious. When he went off to school, we lost contact. The image in my mind didn't fit the person who walked through my door. In front of me stood a handsome, impeccably dressed young man in his early thirties — the picture of success.

I took his hand in both of mine and said, "David, come on in. It's been quite a while. Great to see you!"

I could tell by the look on his face that something was bothering him. "Sit down. How have you been?"

"I'm fine," he replied. "Thanks for seeing me on such short notice."

"It's my pleasure," I said. "So tell me, David, what's on your mind?"

"Rabbi, do you remember in those Sunday morning classes how you would talk about our purpose in this world?"

"Of course."

"Well, Rabbi, I never told you this, but those classes really stayed with me. Back then, I was too young to fully appreciate what you were driving at, but for the longest time I've been meaning to call you up and tell you that your message really had an impact on me."

David went on to explain that while he never actually put into practice what we had studied in those early-morning classes, he always had a strong feeling that what we discussed was deeply and fundamentally true. In his heart he knew that one day he would return to it.

"David, I certainly appreciate hearing that, but somehow I sense that there is something more that's pressing on your mind."

"Right. I kind of wanted to talk to you about that now...about my purpose in life, what my ultimate goals are...."

I looked at him for a moment, taking in his still-youthful enthusiasm, and said, "David, since you moved away we haven't had the opportunity to chat. I would gladly talk to you about anything. But I must ask — why the sudden need to talk about this subject just now?"

"Well, Rabbi, you see, it's this woman. I mean she's great. She is everything I am looking for, we have so much in common, I can really relate to her, and I respect her so much as a person. I feel that I have found the woman with whom I want to spend my life."

"Well, David, I am certainly happy for you. Still, I sense some hesitation on your part." In my heart, I knew what was coming next. How many times had I been here before? A young man comes in to tell me that he has found the love of his life, but she is from a different religion, and his mother, brother, or uncle has sent him to the rabbi to get him to change his mind.

I continued hesitantly, not really wanting to hear the rest. "So, what is the problem?"

"Well, you see...she's kind of...well...I mean, in terms of religion, she's, um...how do I say this? She, um, kind of comes from a different sort of upbringing than I do."

"In what sense?"

"Well, I mean she sort of believes in, I mean she practices...." His voice trailed off.

"David, if this conversation is to be of help to you, we must be open with each other."

"Well, Rabbi, she's observant! You know, a practicing Jew. I mean, she prays and keeps kosher. Every Saturday she goes to synagogue, she doesn't drive, she doesn't turn on lights—the whole nine yards."

I have to admit, he caught me by surprise. This certainly wasn't what I was expecting. "Well, David," I continued, "this is an interesting situation. But what's the problem?"

"The problem is *me*. I mean, I am very interested in her. I can really see myself marrying her. But this religion thing...I mean, Orthodox? I respect you and all...but it's just not for me. I consider myself a religious person, but how can I follow all of those rules and commandments and rituals? I've always prided myself on being a thinking person. How can I get involved in a religious system that makes no sense? Just blindly accept things that I can't understand? It's such a different lifestyle. On the one hand, it seems nice, and I guess if I'd been brought up that way, maybe it wouldn't seem so strange... But, Rabbi, it's just not *me!*"

"Well, David, I have to tell you that I am happy for you. I've heard of far worse things happening to young people looking to settle down."

"I'm also happy, in one sense," David responded, "but my problem is what to do. I was hoping that you could help me sort this out."

"David, I'll be more than glad to do whatever I can to help you. But I hope you realize that this might take us some time."

"Rabbi, whatever it takes...I'm prepared to invest."

"OK," I responded. "Let's get started."

Chapter Three

APPRECIATING OUR WEALTH

Imagine a man who, at age thirty-five, becomes blind. For the next ten years, he does his best to reconstruct his life, but now without sight. Being a fighter, he struggles to create a productive life for himself, and in a real sense he succeeds. One day, his doctor informs him of an experimental procedure that, if successful, would enable him to see again. He is both frightened and exuberant. If it works, he regains his sight. If it fails, he might die.

He gathers together his family to talk it over. After much debate he announces, "I am going ahead with it."

The operation is scheduled. The long-awaited day arrives. Paralyzed with dread, he is wheeled toward the operating room. He is sedated, and he sleeps through the ten-hour operation.

When he wakes up, his first thought is to open his eyes. He prepares himself for the moment when he will find out how he will spend the rest of his life. He musters his courage and flexes his eyelids. They don't move! In a panic, he cries out, "NURSE!"

The nurse calmly explains that his bandages won't come off for at least three more days. So he waits. Each moment is like a decade, each hour a lifetime. Finally, it is time. With his family gathered around, with the doctors and nurses at his side, the surgeon begins removing the gauze. The first bandage comes off, then the second. The surgeon says, "Open your eyes." He does.

And he sees!

For the first time in ten years, he looks out and experiences the sights of this world — and he is struck by it all. Struck by the brilliance of colors and shapes; moved by the beauty and magnificence of all that is now in front of him. He looks out the window and sees a meadow, covered with beautiful, green grass. He sees flowers in full bloom. He looks up and sees a clear blue sky. He sees people, faces, loved ones who have been only images in his mind — the sight of his own children whom he hasn't seen in ten years. Tears well in his eyes as he speaks, "Doctor, what can I say? What can I ever do to repay you for what you have given me, for this magnificent gift of sight? Thank you!"

This type of emotion, this extreme joy and sense of appreciation, is something we should feel regularly. The feeling of elation that this man felt when he regained his sight is something that we can feel on a daily basis — if we go through the process of training ourselves to feel it. We have this most precious, unparalleled gift called sight, and it is something that we are supposed to stop and think about. Not just once in a lifetime, not even once a year, but every day. A part of our spiritual growth is learning to appreciate the gifts that we have. One of the blessings said in the morning thanks God for this most wonderful gift of sight. It was designed to be said with an outpouring of emotion.

We humans are a curious breed. We can have treasures for years, not once thinking of the wealth we have been given, not once stopping to appreciate it, never taking a moment to be thankful for it, until something happens and we lose that gift. Then, it's, "God, why me? Of all the people on the planet, why did You pick me?" Till then there wasn't a moment of reflection. Not one thank-you. Not one word of appreciation. Not even a recognition of it being a gift. Once it is gone, the complaints find their home.

Unfortunately, we don't take the time to think about the many gifts we have. We become so accustomed to them that we almost don't know they exist. How many times do we stop and appreciate that we have legs with which to walk and hands with which to hold? How many mornings do we wake up and just take the time to recognize that we have our health and well-being? How much richer is our life because we have eyes with which to see, fingers with which to feel, ears with which to hear, a tongue with which to taste, and a nose with which to smell?

Each of these senses was created by God, created with much wisdom and forethought, created for a specific intention so that we can live a fuller, richer, more complete life — so that we should enjoy our stay on this planet. There is so much about this world that we live in that was custom-designed, specifically for our enjoyment. But it takes focus and training to appreciate the riches we possess.

As an example, let's take a step back from life as we know it and imagine the very moment that Hashem created the world.

Picture, if you will, vast emptiness. Nothing. The absolute absence of anything.

This isn't easy to do. I remember when my daughter was six years old and we were discussing *Bereishis* (Creation), there was one issue that she couldn't come to terms with.

"Abba," she said to me, "I understand that before Hashem created the world there was nothing, not even light and dark, but what color was it?"

The difficulty she was feeling was that we are so used to the world as it is, that the concept of *before creation* is difficult for us to fathom. The idea of the absence of anything — before there was a world, before there was even matter or space or any substance to hold it in — is very difficult for us corporeal beings to deal with. We keep falling back to our way of viewing things in a physical setting, and absolute void has no place in our world.

Still, let's try for a moment to envision a vast, empty nothingness. There is no space, no matter, there isn't even time, because time only exists in a physical world. And creation begins — out of nothing, because there is nothing; from nowhere, because there is no place. At this absolute first moment in time, God brings forth matter, the very building blocks of creation, then darkness and light — not even separated, but intermingled, a patch of light here, a flash of darkness there. Next comes the heavens and earth, then the planets and stars, the fish in the sea, the birds in the sky, and all of the animals of the earth, and then on the final day, at almost the last moment of creation, man.

Every part of creation has to be thought out. There are no givens. There is no imitating or accepting the status quo, because before creation there is nothing to imitate or use as a model. Every part and every element of this world has to be planned and designed from scratch. When we take this huge leap of understanding, we can begin to see the abundance of goodness that God has bestowed upon the world.

Let's start with something basic — color. The world is fantastically rich in color, with so many gradations, shades, and hues.

Color is something that we take for granted. Of course, there is color in the world; it was always there.

God created this thing that we call color, and He put it in the world for a particular reason: so that we should enjoy what we see. The world didn't have to be this way. If God was only concerned with functionality — with creating a world that could be used — black and white would have sufficed. We would still be able to recognize objects and people, even shadows and depth, within the spectrum of the gray scale. If you have ever seen a TV program from the early 1960s, it was just that — black and white — and it did a fine job. You could still experience the full human drama within the gray scale. But it lacked a dimension — it was flat, and so it wasn't as enjoyable. Hashem wants us to enjoy this world, so He created the entity called color.

Look out on a fall day and see the trees in their glory, the seemingly endless array of reds, oranges, and brilliant yellows form a magnificent tapestry stretching across the mountains. Look out at the sun as it sets and you can see the most radiant show of color, the full spectrum of an artist's palette, painted against a powdery gray backdrop.

If the world was created for practical reasons only, all of the beauty that we witness wouldn't have to be. God put it all here, from magnificent floral scenes, to exotic sea life; from the glory of the night sky, to the clear aqua green of the ocean; from a flower in bloom, to the plume of a jungle parrot; all of the pomp and ceremony of a sunrise — a world created in Technicolor. Why create it that way? Why not make it all black and white? Keep it plain, keep it simple. Why go through all of the effort? The answer is for one reason — so that man should enjoy. God did all of this for us so that we should look out at the world and enjoy its beauty.

This is only one of the pleasures that we enjoy but take for granted. What about food? Food is something that we need to maintain our energy levels and health. If its only function were nutrition and nothing more, then all the foods that we eat should taste like soggy cardboard. Yet they don't. There are so many different and varied types of foods, each with its own unique flavor, texture, and aroma. Why? Why not make it all taste like oatmeal? Again, for one reason: so that man should enjoy. So that eating, which we have to do, shouldn't be a chore but rather delightful. Taste is something that God added solely for our benefit — for our pleasure.

An awful lot of thought went into creating the different foods we eat. I once heard Rabbi Avigdor Miller, *zt"l*, describe an orange. He said that when you peel an orange, inside there are wedges. If you look closely, each of these wedges is surrounded by a thin membrane. When you pull back the membrane and look inside, you will see many tiny sacs. Inside each of those sacs is the juice of the orange. Now why did God create an orange in that manner, with thousands of little sacks? The reason is because it further enhances our enjoyment. Did you ever see one of those children's candies with a liquid center? They're advertised with the slogan, "Bite in for a burst of flavor." When you bite into an orange, you also get a burst of flavor. Because the juice of the orange is contained within those many small sacs, when you bite into it, there is a release of juice in the form of a burst, and that adds to the enjoyment of eating the orange. God created those sacs so that there would be another dimension to our enjoyment. The sensation of eating an orange would be different without this feature. It still would have tasted delicious, but this is an additional aspect that God wanted us to enjoy, so He designed an orange in this way.

Did you ever wonder why Delicious apples are red on the outside?

It's for the same reason that laundry detergents come packaged in bright colors. Procter & Gamble spent millions of dollars on research to determine which color has the greatest eye appeal. They have done countless studies proving that putting Tide in a bright, neon-orange container will result in more sales. Consumers prefer it — it has more eye appeal — and shoppers will reach for it before the other detergents. Cheerios has been in that same yellow box for sixty years now! Studies show that that shade of yellow sells more boxes of cereal than any other color. People simply like it.

So too, God made some apples red because they are nicer to look at, and that makes the process of eating an apple more enjoyable. As any chef will explain, the presentation adds much to the enjoyment of the dish. Therefore, God designed that the foods we eat have eye appeal so as to enhance our experience of eating. Keep in mind that food is only needed to provide nourishment. Any other feature we find is there because God had a specific reason for it; many of those were created simply so that we should have greater pleasure and enjoyment.

Here is another example: what happens when you bite into an apple? You don't get the same burst of flavor that you get when you bite into an orange. You get a crunch. Why? Why not design all fruit the same? The reason why an apple is crunchy is because it is *fun* to crunch on food. That's why your local supermarket has an entire aisle, seventy-five feet long, floor to ceiling, stocked with breakfast cereals, each one bragging that they're crispier then the next: "Crispy," "Crispier," "Crispiest," "Ours is so crispy we even include ear plugs!"

Why is each food manufacturer trying to get you to think that their cereal is the crispiest? Because it's fun to bite into something crunchy; we like that sensation when we eat. So General Mills makes their cereals crunchy, and when God made apples, He designed the cells to form hard walls so that when we bite into it we get a texture that provides a crunch. It didn't have to be that way. God designed it that way so that we should enjoy it.

For the life of me I still can't figure out why bananas are mushy! But I guess sometimes some people are in the mood for that soft, squishy texture.

What about aroma? Have you ever found yourself in a restaurant, and as the waiter brought out your favorite dish, your mouth began watering at the sight of it? But you had a cold, and when you began eating it, somehow it didn't taste right. You just couldn't enjoy it. Scientists now recognize that most of our sense of taste comes through smell. When God created food, He added this dimension of wonderful aromas to enhance our taste experience. Each of the different foods that we enjoy not only has a different taste and texture, it also has a markedly different smell, which contributes to our total enjoyment.

Did you ever notice that when you peel an orange, as you break the outer skin, a fine mist of juice sprays up? The next time you peel one, pay attention and you will see that the skin has tiny bubbles in it. When they break open, they create that fine mist that emits the delicate aroma of an orange. Why did God go through all of the effort to design those microencapsulated specks of juice in the skin? For one reason, so that when you peel an orange you will smell the fragrance and hunger for it. When you hunger for food, your enjoyment of it is increased.

It wasn't enough that the flavor of the orange was made so special with a mix of sweetness and tang, and that the wedges were made up of little sacs to provide that "burst of flavor." Maybe we wouldn't be quite hungry enough, so God designed these tiny bubbles in the skin to further increase our enjoyment. It didn't have to be that way. To get our daily dose of vitamin C, we could have done just as well without all of the enhancements. But God wanted to add pleasure to our eating.

We were given so many different and varied forms of food. From roast beef to chicken, to hot dogs, to avocados, to yogurt, to bananas, to pickles, to olives, to strawberries, to salmon — so many assorted spices and flavors, all different and varied. If you look at a typical salad, you will see so many different shapes, textures, and flavors: tomatoes, cucumbers, peppers, lettuce, mushrooms — each one distinct, each one contributing its unique qualities to the whole. Why? Why create them that way? Why not make them all brown like beans and taste like potatoes? The reason is because that wouldn't have been fun. The food we eat comes in so many assorted flavors and textures, each one appealing to a different element of our tastes. God preplanned and created all of this for us to enjoy.

Yet how often do we actually take the time to enjoy the foods that we eat? How much attention do we pay to taking pleasure from the sights that we see? It takes training and concentration to consciously choose to enjoy the life that we lead. If we do, we will see a tremendous amount of detail and concern that God put in for man to enjoy. And we will see an amazing demonstration of the kindness that God shows to man.

After I finished sharing these ideas, David looked up, smiling.

"I have to admit," he said, "that I have never focused on the amount of good God put in this world for us to enjoy. I certainly see how thinking about these types of things help a person live a richer, happier life...but what does this have to do with my question?"

"David," I said, "all this brings me to an important point. May I ask you a question?"

"Sure."

"Are you happy?"

Chapter Four

OF COURSE I'M HAPPY. AREN'T I?

"Am I happy?"

"Yes, are you happy?"

"I like to think that I am..." David responded. "I guess it depends on what you mean by happy."

"The reason I ask that question," I said, "is because we live in times when there is an increased emphasis on having fun, on being happy, on living life to its fullest. And it seems that we have all we need to do just that. After centuries of suffering, man seems to have finally found freedom from oppression. At least in the free world, we live in open and accepting societies and enjoy unprecedented human rights and prosperity. We benefit from amazing health advances and live within safe borders; we no longer fear marauders or the Black Plague; we enjoy an advanced social structure and have a vast array of technological wonders at our fingertips. We should finally be happy.

"Yet, in my encounters with people, I don't find this to be true. I meet with a lot of people. And, sure, everyone's initial response is, 'Life is great, couldn't be better.' But when you get past the social civilities, there's a whole other world brewing inside. The truth is that most people I meet aren't really happy. When you sit them down to talk, when they come into my office and we get into what is really on their minds, few are happy. So many individuals who are financially secure, holding good jobs and important positions, people who enjoy great social acceptance and status, aren't happy — but why? We have so much. We enjoy so many luxuries, we are so wealthy. It would seem that simply by living in this generation we should be happy beyond description. We boast of greater prosperity today than any other generation that has inhabited this planet. Certainly, in terms of luxuries and comforts, we are unrivaled in the course of history. Yet we're not happy. I believe there is a root cause of this, and once we understand that root cause, we can retrain ourselves to enjoy life. But before we do that, I would like to focus for a minute on the abundance of wealth that we enjoy.

"My grandmother grew up in Poland before the First World War. She told me that her family was considered well-off — they lived in a two-room house. That meant two rooms. One for the parents, and one where the family ate, played, did chores, cooked, bathed, cleaned their clothes, and slept. That was it, two rooms. Period. And believe me, the rooms weren't large, and the families weren't small.

"Today, when we go on vacation and 'rough it' by putting the whole family — parents and two kids — in one motel room, it's cute and cozy...for an evening. But that was the amount of space that people lived in with all their possessions — all the time. That was home. On floors made of dirt, with furniture consisting of the barest table and a few chairs, with wood-burning fireplaces that had to be stocked by chopping trees, they lived. With walls filled with cracks that let the cold air of winter in but held the sweltering heat of summer; driving a horse to the market and bathing only on special occasions; without phones, without TV, without running water or electricity, people lived. Regular people, our people, our grandparents, or great-grandparents, lived.

"We aren't any different than they were. They walked, ate, slept, and breathed as we do. They weren't born on a different planet, and they didn't live a thousand years ago. Yet their lives were so different from ours that it's difficult for us to even imagine ourselves in that setting.

"I had a great-aunt Perel who came over from Poland before my grandmother did. When my grandmother first came to visit, Tanta Perel said to her in an excited voice, 'You must see this. You won't believe your eyes! Our new building has a bathroom in the apartment itself!' It was a standard of luxury that she couldn't even imagine.

"While it may sound like ancient history to us, it wasn't that long ago that people used outhouses. In the freezing cold of winter, they would don a coat, go out to the back, and there find a bare hut. This was how they lived.

"There was no such thing as cars and planes and buses. If you had somewhere to go, you got into a horse-drawn wagon and bumped along a stone road for hours till your insides wanted to come out. There was no such thing as smooth roads and highways. Even smooth walls were something unheard of.

"Even heat was a luxury only for the rich. My father had a friend who grew up in a cold part of Eastern Europe; he had a handy way of telling whether it was a cold morning. There is a Jewish tradition to wash one's hands immediately upon awaking in the morning. Many people leave a vessel filled with water next to their bed so they can wash as soon as they get up. In the early morning, before this man got out of bed, he would look in the vessel — if it had iced over, he knew it was a cold day!

"Water doesn't turn to ice at fifty-eight degrees. And not at forty-eight either. He slept in the very room that the water froze in! Now we set our thermostats to a comfy seventy degrees, and if it goes below sixty-two, we complain — 'Hey, it's freezing in here!' Did you ever have your furnace go out? You called the heating company, and they said they'd have someone there by the morning. When the house temperature got down into the fifties, you went to sleep at your neighbors, saying, 'How could anyone possibly survive in fifty degrees?!'

"Yet people did survive — people who were no different from you or me, and at temperatures well below fifty degrees.

"We also enjoy material possessions that two or three generations ago were unimaginable. If you walk down an aisle in Wal-Mart, everything you could possibly want is available to be had. In whatever color, shape, and texture we like, it is there for us to buy. And for the most part, we have money to buy it with.

"To give you an illustration, I gave a talk on this topic, and after the lecture a woman came over to tell me an incident. She was friendly with a new immigrant — a Russian woman. She took her new friend on their first outing to a large supermarket. When this Russian immigrant walked into the produce section and saw the abundance and plenty on display, she was so overcome with emotion that she fainted. In all of her years she had never seen so much food, so readily available. During the Communist regime it was considered a regular part of the day to wait for hours on line for food and often end up with nothing because there wasn't enough for everyone. Now, if we are held up for ten minutes at the checkout counter we already start looking for a new grocery store.

"Here's another example. If you live in a house built before World War II, you probably noticed that no matter how large it is, there's never enough closet space. The home might have sizable rooms, plenty of bedrooms, and lots of living space, but tiny, undersized closets. Why didn't they build closets to match the size of the house?

"Because the house was built for people living in those days. No one then would dream that we would own the amount of clothing that we do. I spoke to a woman who grew up in the 1930s, and she told me she had two dresses: one for weekdays and one for Shabbos. She wasn't poor. That was considered normal.

"Today, each member of the family owns racks and racks of clothing: suits, shirts, slacks, skirts, sweaters, winter coats, summer jackets, light fall coats, ties, belts, pocketbooks, and matching accessories, not to mention shoes. My *rebbi*, Rabbi A. H. Leibowitz, *zt"l*, grew up in America in the 1920s. When he was a young boy, the soles of the only pair of shoes he owned developed large holes, and he didn't have the heart to ask his father for the twenty-five cents that it cost to have a shoemaker repair them. So he figured out his own solution. He placed a piece of cardboard inside each shoe so that his socks wouldn't rub out on the concrete while he walked. This worked well until the first rainy day, when he walked outside and right into a puddle. Splash! His new soles were gone.

"Do we know anyone today who doesn't own a number of pairs of shoes? Black, blue, and brown — some for casual wear, others for dress. Gotta have at least one pair for running, another for basketball, and still others for bowling. Do you play golf? If so, only an entirely separate wardrobe is fitting, and Heaven forefend to play tennis in basketball shoes!

"If we were to describe our wealth to people of a different generation, I don't think they would believe us. Kings in prior times didn't enjoy the luxuries that we take for granted. If you look at portraits of King George, the monarch of England before the Revolutionary War, you'll see him sitting on his throne in the comfort of his palace wearing layer upon layer of robes, topped off by a fur covering. Did you ever wonder why he was wearing all of those layers? The reason is that it was mighty cold in the king's palace! The King of England, with all of his wealth, had to keep warm by huddling up to a smoky fireplace that heated only the part of his body that was facing it, not the rest of him. His Highness walked through dimly lit, dank hallways at night. He slept on a mattress stuffed with feathers (with no chiropractors around to care for a back aching from sinking down into thirty-six inches of duck feathers). And when his brother, the Duke, was getting married, traveling to the wedding meant enduring a backbreaking carriage ride for the better part of a week. His crown jewels couldn't buy him the smallest luxuries that we take for granted today.

"The reality is that we are wealthy beyond belief. We enjoy comforts and abundance that are historically unprecedented. And we aren't speaking about the captains of industry or the extremely affluent. The average taxpaying citizens of today live in opulence and splendor that previous generations couldn't even dream about.

"And what about the technological advances that we enjoy today? A friend of mine was flying into New York City, and after touching down, the plane stopped a distance from the terminal. The flight attendant announced that there would be a slight delay as they waited for the walkway to be wheeled over. The passengers watched as a technician maneuvered a mobile gangplank into place. The person sitting next to my friend remarked, 'Look at the wonders of technology. They even have moving walkways!'

"My friend was flabbergasted. They had just been traveling five hundred miles an hour at an altitude of thirty-five thousand feet. No cables, no wires — flying in the air. And this person was astonished by a movable gangplank! What happened to the sense of amazement that man has so mastered the laws of gravity that he can fly? What happened to the sense of astonishment of traveling across the world in a matter of hours? Ah, that's yesterday's news. We are so used to it that we take it for granted. In reality, the luxuries that we enjoy due to technological advances are fantastic: from iPods to e-mail, from an array of frozen and canned goods to microwave ovens, from laptop computers to GPS devices that guide us to the most far-flung destinations.

"In short, we are wealthy beyond belief. We have riches that far exceed our needs. As a society, as a nation, and as individuals, we enjoy prosperity and abundance, and benefit from creature comforts that were unthinkable a generation ago. Everything is so readily available, so accessible, so easy to obtain. And so I have one question: Now that we have so much, are we happy?

"For centuries, all that man desired was freedom from tyranny and a homeland where he could raise his family in liberty and safety. Armies went to war for it, entire generations sacrificed all that they had for it, and we now have it. We are there. We have finally arrived. Living in a free society with almost unlimited opportunity, we are easily able to find sustenance and enjoy unheard-of wealth. We have it all. But are we happy? Now that we are there, is it all that we thought it would be? Is this the dream that we were seeking? Are we any happier today than our ancestors were in previous generations?"

When I finished speaking, I let my words sink in for a while.

Then David responded, "You definitely have a point, we don't adequately appreciate the wealth and luxuries that we enjoy. But wouldn't you agree that, all in all, most people today are happier than their ancestors were in previous generations?"

"Truthfully," I responded, "it's difficult to compare how happy one generation is compared to another, but here is one barometer.

"Richard Easterlin, an economic historian at the University of Southern California, conducted an eye-opening study in which he compared the relationship of increasing income to happiness. He found that although the gross domestic product per capita in the USA has more than doubled in the past half century, there has been absolutely no improvement in the percentage of happy people. We have more than twice the amount of goods available to each consumer, as compared to fifty years ago — twice as many cars, twice as many refrigerators, twice as many homes — yet we aren't any happier. He goes on to say, 'Even though each generation has more than its predecessor, each generation wants more.' He points out that one of the most enduring cultural beliefs is that a 20 percent increase in our income would make us perfectly happy, but it simply isn't true. No sooner do we get that 20 percent increase then we need more, and we enter into an unending cycle.

"This brings us to an odd phenomenon. It seems that there is an inherent cultural belief that money will solve all problems. Do you remember the song 'If I Were a Rich Man' from *Fiddler on the Roof*?

> *If I were a rich man*
> *I wouldn't have to work hard,*
> *dee, dee, dee, dee, dee dee, deedle, deedle, dum*
> *All day long I'd deedle, deedle, dum,*
> *if I were a wealthy man…*

"Even though it's hard to believe, there is still an inherent cultural belief that money will solve all of my problems. *If only I were a millionaire — wow, life would be great! All of my problems would be solved. I would be so happy.* I am speaking about intelligent, thinking people who somehow get caught up in this myth — in this never-ending pursuit of wealth — all the while thinking, at least in the back of their minds, that more money means more happiness. But it doesn't work, because no sooner do they get more then they need even more than that.

"This point is illustrated by a study of major lottery winners, people who won significant fortunes. Within one year of winning the jackpot, eighty percent were back at work. Eighty percent! That means all of those people who for years were saying, 'Just wait till I win the jackpot. Just one big one, and I'm gone! You won't see my face in this joint again.' But within a year they were back, often at the same job they left. This is especially intriguing because many of the winners weren't in high-satisfaction employment. Often, they were typical working-class people who drove cabs, waited on tables, or were employed in factories.

"To put this into perspective, let's imagine Bob, the UPS driver. He hates his job, talks about quitting all the time. His favorite expression is, 'A bad day at fishing is better than a good day at work.'

"Each week Bob sets out with a dollar and a dream to buy himself a lottery ticket, and waits for his numbers to come in. Then one day, lo and behold, Bob wins! And he wins big; enough money that he doesn't have to work a day in his life again.

"What happens?

"First, Bob buys himself that ultimate fishing boat. Then he buys every imaginable lure and casting system known to man. Then he's off on a world cruise. Life could not be better. Day after carefree day...

"From Morocco to Tunisia to Egypt, he covers the sun-scorched deserts on camelback. Then, dodging donkeys and goats, he makes his way through the dusty streets of Istanbul to savor the dazzling bazaars. A quick stop over at the Turkish baths, and onward to the Caribbean: Barbados, Curaçao, and Costa Rica.

"But then a funny thing happens. Bob gets bored. Been there, done that. Kayaked the Amazon river, ATVed up the pyramids. Now what? Back to work he marches. Back to the same brown truck, back to the same brown pants and socks, back to the very same route. Once again, Bob is picking up packages and dropping them off.

"What happened? All he needed to truly enjoy life was a taste of wealth — and he got it. What could be better? He had clearly believed that with more than enough money his life would be completely different. Yet now that he had it, his life hadn't magically changed. He didn't suddenly find the potion of unending joy and eternal bliss he was seeking.

"The compelling part of these studies is that it's difficult to find any correlation between increased income and greater happiness. And while we all *sort of* know that, we live our lives as if it weren't true. We have been socialized into the mindless acceptance of the belief that 'more money equals more happiness.' But it doesn't work. The money looks so tempting, so alluring; it seems that it will fill all of our needs and wants. But at the end of the day, it left Bob just as hungry — not for more money or more luxuries — but for something else. He just isn't satisfied.

"Why? Why doesn't it make him happy? It was all he ever wanted. It was all he ever dreamed about. Now that he has it, why can't he just be happy?

"The question we have to deal with is: Why? What is it? I have so much, why aren't I happy? I have a great job, a fantastic social life. I have unimaginable conveniences and luxuries. I have a home with straight walls and heat, with carpet in every room. Even my car is air-conditioned so that I shouldn't suffer while I drive around on an air-cushioned suspension system. I own the finest sound system, and I won't settle for anything less than the highest quality CD recordings — it has to sound live. I have wealth and well-being that is simply astounding. And yet I am not happy. But why not?

"And what makes this question even more profound is that God created a custom-made world with so much thought and focus, all for my enjoyment. All of the beauty of creation, from the brilliance of a sunset, to the lushness of a tropical garden, all of the colors and hues, are there so that I should benefit. All of the smells that we experience, from the gentle fragrance of a rose, to the aroma of roast beef, were put there for my benefit. All of the different colors, textures, and flavors of food are all there for me to enjoy — yet I don't enjoy them. Why not? What is missing?

"What is missing is that all of these things only feed one part of me. Money and material possessions, honor and prestige, careers and promotions only feed one dimension of who I truly am. If man were a horse, then the formula for his happiness would be simple: put him in a meadow, give him a bag of oats and a nice mare, and he would be happy.

"The problem is that man isn't merely a horse. There is a part of man that isn't satisfied, can't be satisfied, with food and drink. There is a part of man that aspires for more out of life and searches for significance and purpose. This part needs to live a life that matters and has consequence; it seeks out true meaning in life. Because of this, trying to make man happy by giving him more physical pleasure alone just doesn't work. It can't work because it ignores one of the most basic needs of man. It is like drinking when you are hungry — for a while, the feeling of being bloated subdues the hunger pangs, but within minutes the hunger returns, and now more intense than before.

"We live in very sophisticated times, and it seems that we know all of the answers to mankind's problems. Yet it seems as if we have forgotten some of the basic tenets of being human. It's almost as if we have lost some of the very underpinnings of life, and so with all of our material gains we just aren't happy. To regain these, we need a new level of understanding that begins with the most basic issues about being human: understanding the inner workings of the human personality."

I looked up and saw that it was dark outside. I realized that we had gotten lost in conversation. I hadn't intended to spend so much time on this subject, but I feel pretty passionate about it. I turned to David, and said, "Our work is going to take more than a few quick sessions. The issues that we need to deal with aren't about rituals or customs; they're about understanding man and his place in this universe. To do that we will need a strong understanding of why God put us on this planet, and what He wants from us. And even more, we will need to deal with the meaning of life itself.

"My suggestion would be that we make up a time each week to meet. Does Tuesday at two work for you?"

"Sure, that's fine," David said as he stood up. "Rabbi, I want to thank you. I have a feeling that this is going to prove to be a meaningful experience."

"I certainly hope so, David," I answered.

Chapter Five

THE VOICE INSIDE

When David returned the next week, I asked him if he'd had a chance to think about what we had discussed.

"I sure did. But while I admit that you have piqued my curiosity, I'm not sure I know where you're headed, Rabbi."

"In what sense?"

"Well, let's start with this: I find fascinating your observation that God added many features to this world so that we should enjoy our stay. I found myself thinking about some of your examples; I don't know if I can ever eat an orange the same way again! And I certainly agree that there has to be more to a person's life than only focusing on his own enjoyment. Yet I'm not sure that I accept your premise — that unless a person finds meaning in his life, he can't be happy. In fact, I could see a person living a happier life not having to deal with these types of issues. Imagine a person who never has to deal with questions like, 'What is the meaning of life?' and 'What is my purpose in the world?' He would find life itself so much more enjoyable just sort of taking one day at time, dealing with life as it unfolds, unencumbered by any of these nagging issues. It seems that these questions themselves bring a person to unhappiness, and prevent him from enjoying life."

I looked at David for a moment before responding. "On the surface it might seem so," I said. "The problem is that God didn't design the human to function that way. And when you try to use an object in a manner different than its intended purpose, it leads to disharmony. You see, God created us in a very specific manner, almost with an internal guiding system. If a person lives his life in accordance with that purpose, then he will find peace, tranquility, and harmony. If he leads life at cross purposes with his inner self, he will find himself in discordance, because something is off. He isn't attuned to his internal compass, he isn't aligned with himself, and as such he can't be happy."

"Did God create us to be happy?" David asked.

"Whether God made us for that reason or not," I said, "a good barometer of whether a person's life is in balance is his state of happiness. If a person is truly happy, that is a sign that he is at peace with himself. The opposite is also true. I've met many people who appear successful, yet wake up one morning and just don't want to get out of bed. And the worst part is that they don't know why! This person may seek help — by going to his analyst or to his psychologist — and search for a solution. The real problem is that there is no problem; there is no apparent cause for his unhappiness. All systems are go, everything in his life is in place, and for all intents and purposes he should be happy. Yet he isn't.

"David, I would like to share something with you. For many people the reason that they are unhappy is because they are not in sync with themselves. There is a Voice Inside that doesn't let them rest, that isn't satisfied with the way they are living their life, and that Voice speaks up and unsettles their entire existence.

"Do you know what I mean by this Voice Inside?"

"Yes. Well, sort of…"

"Let me show you what I'm referring too. Have you ever heard of something called Jewish guilt?"

I got a chuckle out of David, and then he said, "Sure have."

"While we tend to think of guilt as negative," I said, "it is fundamental to our proper functioning. Let me show you what I mean. Have you ever had a really nagging moral dilemma, where you really wanted to do something but knew it was wrong? Not clearly wrong in the sense of a crime, more of something that we would call a white lie, something almost innocent sounding, but not quite that.

"Picture this: The law firm you work for is involved in a merger between two publicly traded major corporations. You're having lunch with an old school buddy, Tom, and the conversation turns to the merger. Much to your surprise, he works for an investment firm.

"'David,' he says, 'this is gold! I have a client who would pay a king's ransom for that kind of information, if you could just get me a few details, even the asking price and when it is going to happen, it would be so valuable!'

"'Wait a minute, Tom…what do you mean?' you respond. 'That's confidential client information. You are asking me to be involved in insider trading. It's illegal; I could be disbarred. I mean, people go to prison for that kind of thing. Forget it. No way.'

"So you leave the restaurant with a kind of queasy feeling inside, but not giving much thought to what happened.

"Later that day, the phone rings. It's Tom.

"'Hey, David.'

"'Yeah, how are you doing?'

"'Listen, David, I spoke with my client. He told me that if I could get him some information, he would wire transfer a hundred thousand dollars into my account by tomorrow morning. What do you say, old buddy? We can split it fifty-fifty. Think about it. *Think about it — no risk, easy money.* I'll call you later.' And he hangs up.

"As you hear him click off, you feel a sinking feeling in your stomach. Fifty thousand dollars sure could go a long way. And as a lawyer you know full well that there's no way in the world that you would get caught for this kind of thing — one phone conversation, no records, no way to tie it back to you. Besides, it is too petty for anyone to get excited about. Just an easy fifty grand.

"And so you begin that fight, that battle between two opposing forces, between what you want, and that Voice Inside that knows what is right.

"*Come on,* you think, *who gets hurt? These are huge corporations; they have billions of dollars in assets. The only thing that's going to happen is that Tom's client will know about the merger, so he'll buy a block of stock. It's not like we're dealing with some huge amount of money that will change the market. He makes out well, Tom and I make out well. No one gets hurt. Why not?*

"But that Voice Inside isn't buying. It says. 'Come on, David, you know it's wrong. It's using information that you were trusted with; it's confidential for a reason. Besides, it violates the law.'

"'So what?' you respond, 'Where's the crime? It's just using some information that I happen to have.'

"'David,' that Voice says, 'it's against the law of the land. You took an oath to uphold that law. How can you now violate that law for your own interests?'

"And this goes on all night, this conversation between the two voices inside you. You barely sleep that night.

"Now, David, let's take this a step further. Let's imagine that our little episode doesn't have a Hollywood ending. Let's imagine you go through with the deal. The next day you call up your old buddy, utter a couple of brief sentences, and it's done. True to his word, within two hours fifty thousand dollars is deposited into your account.

"Now what? Initially you feel pretty good. After all, that was the easiest money you ever made. But at dinner that evening, you just don't feel quite yourself, something is bugging you.

"Lisa looks at you and says, 'David, is everything OK?'

"'Yeah, just have something on my mind. Nothing...big.'

"'Do you want to talk about it?'

"'No, it's just something I have to sort out.'

"'You sure? You really don't look good.'

"'No, I'm OK, really. Just something I need to work out.'

That night when you get home, you have little peace. That Voice Inside your head starts in.

'David, why did you do that? You don't lack money. You have a good job. You know why you did it? It was greed. Plain old, simple greed.'

"'Oh, come on, now,' you answer. 'I'm thinking of getting married, and fifty grand can go a long way toward a down payment on a house.'

"But the Voice doesn't stop.

"'David,' it says, 'What's next? Cheating on taxes, maybe a little falsifying of documents? Where does it end?'

"'Oh, please,' you answer back. 'It was a little innocent sharing of information, that's all.'

'No, it wasn't, David,' the voice continues. 'How come you were so embarrassed when Lisa asked you about it? How come you clammed right up? It's because it was wrong — and you know it.'

'Come on now, no one was hurt, no harm was done,' you shoot back.

'Yeah, but David, it was wrong. You broke the law. Honestly, I'm disappointed in you.'

'Leave me alone!'

'No, David, it was wrong and you know it! You did something that you shouldn't have done.'

'So I did, so what? So I broke a law, who cares? People do things like that a thousand time a day.'

'Yeah, but David, you aren't like those people. You don't do those kinds of things. You should be ashamed of yourself.'

'Leave me alone! What are you, my mother or something? Just bug off, and leave me alone!' you scream.

"The problem is that the Voice won't leave you alone. You can try running from it. You can try hiding from it. You can try to distract yourself, but when you are alone, when your busy work is done, that Voice returns to haunts you. And you can't escape it, because that Voice is you. It's that part of you that is noble and good and proper. It's that part of you that is embarrassed by what you did. It's that part of you that only wants to do what is right, that strives for greatness."

I let my words sink in. Then I turned back to David and said, "David, when my children were young I got to see this 'Voice Inside' very clearly. As adults we are quite skilled at hiding our inner mo- tives — even from ourselves — but little children are transparent. I can still remember when my oldest daughter was five years old and she did something that she wasn't supposed to. My wife would look at her and say. 'Sarah, did you take a cookie?'

"Silence.

"'Sarah, did you take a cookie from the cabinet?'

"More silence. Then her little voice would pipe up and say, 'No, Mommy, I didn't.'

"'Sarah, look at me and tell me: Did. You. Take. A. Cookie?'

"Invariably, Sarah would then gaze at the floor, her face would first turn red and then white, her lips would twist into a wry smile, and she would say, 'Yes, Mommy, I did.'

"David, at that moment, it was very important to this little girl to be able to say that she didn't take that cookie. She very much wanted to eat that cookie, and didn't want the consequences of having taken it without permission. The simple solution was to lie, to simply say, 'No, Mommy, I didn't take it.' And she desperately wanted to say just that. But she couldn't. As much as she wanted to, there was a Voice Inside her that told her, 'But you did take it. You can't lie to Mommy.'

"Children are innocent, and so that Voice Inside speaks out clearly. It tells them what is right and what is wrong. As we get older, something interesting happens. While that voice inside remains as potent as ever, we develop a counter voice that allows us to overpower the Voice Inside. When my daughter turned nine or ten, she was able to lie. When that Voice Inside said, 'What you are saying isn't true,' she was now stronger and able to say, 'Just be quiet, I am in charge here. I know I took that cookie, but I am going to say that I didn't.' And at that age, when my wife would stare her down, there was no nervous sort of giggle that gave her away. She was capable of looking my wife in the eye, and saying, 'No, I didn't do it.'

"David, don't get me wrong. I feel blessed to have wonderful children who are honest, straightforward people. But there was a difference. When they were young, they almost didn't have a choice, they could be so easily flushed out. As they matured, they had to make a conscious choice to be honest, because they had acquired the ability to lie. They had acquired the ability to overpower that Voice Inside. Even though that inner tension was still there, they now had the capacity to act against that Voice.

"We see the power of this Voice in other situations. They aren't popular now in trials, but there was a time when criminals were given lie detector tests. Picture a hardened criminal, a man who spent years making his living by lying, cheating, stealing, living a life of crime — clearly a person without a conscience. He is caught with incriminating evidence, but not quite enough to make an airtight case. So they bring him into a room, hook him up to some monitors, and begin asking him a series of questions.

"'What's your name?' 'How old are you?' 'Where were you born?' 'Where do you live?' While he answers these baseline questions, a technician is noting the movement of indicators that measure his pulse, blood pressure, breathing rate, and perspiration.

"Then the questions change. 'Have you ever committed a crime?'

"'No.' All four indicators take a sharp upswing.

"'Have you ever been arrested?'

"'No.' The indicators shoot up further.

"Then comes that critical question: 'On the fifteenth of December, were you at the scene of the crime?'

"'No.' The indicators all but jump off the chart.

"Now, let's understand what is happening here. We have a mature individual who is fully aware that the information found out here will be used against him in a court of law. He recognizes the consequences, and he is also quite aware that when he comes into this room, he is going to be asked certain questions. He might very well have practiced the answers for days. Yet when he answers those questions, there is a noticeable, physiological reaction. He can lie to the court. He can lie to the District Attorney. He can even to lie to himself. But there is that Voice Inside of him that knows the truth. And when he answers what he knows to be a lie, there is an internal conflict that flares up when that Voice says, 'You know full well that you stole that merchandise.' Even as he is saying to himself, 'Just deny it, keep calm and tell them the story,' that Voice Inside says, 'But it's not true. It didn't happen that way.' He may try to squelch it, but that conflict is so strong that it has a physical effect on him, an effect so noticeable that a polygraph can measure the internal conflict.

"That Voice Inside is something we were given at birth; we were created with an inner sense of right and wrong, an inborn understanding of what is appropriate and what is not. When we do what is right, that Voice lets us know it, and we feel good about ourselves. If we do something wrong, that Voice lets us know it as well.

"I'm sure you have heard of attorneys raising a defense based on their client's not knowing any better. I have read of cases of inner-city teenagers being defended with a line of reasoning that went something like this: 'Since he was a youngster, violence has been a way of life for him. Since he began developing any sense of the world, all he has experienced is the law of the jungle — eat or be eaten. Because we can't expect better from such a young man, the court must have mercy.'

"David, I consider myself a compassionate person, and I do feel for the plight of teens raised in such intolerable circumstances. But when a fifteen-year-old pulls out a gun and shoots down a man in cold blood because he wanted the fellow's leather jacket, that argument just doesn't cut it.

"You don't have to graduate Harvard Divinity School to understand that stealing is wrong. You don't have to attend seminars about developing your spiritual dimension to know that murder is wrong. God created man with an inner sense of right and wrong, an ability to decide in each situation the correct course of behavior.

"We may be tempted to go against this Voice, we may wish to ignore it, but that Voice Inside exists in all humans. And intuitively, without any outside influences, our youth understand that it is wrong to steal and murder. Just like the bird was created with an inner sense to find a worm, and the cat instinctively knows to hunt for mice, man was given a higher instinct — that of right and wrong. The only question is: Will he listen to it?

"This Voice plays out in our inner self whether we want it to or not. We may not have asked for it, we may not welcome it, but it is present deep within us.

"As an example: Henry Ford, the inventor of the assembly line, was a brilliant innovator and successful businessman. And while he won fame and fortune in the world of car production, it seems that he didn't fare quite as well as a human being. In fact, he used to brag that he never did anything for anyone but himself, and he often boasted of strictly adhering to this 'principle.'

"Nevertheless, the story is told that one day, while he was walking with a friend, he heard yelps of pain coming from a nearby field. It seems that a dog had gotten caught in a barbed-wire fence and couldn't free itself. Henry Ford stopped, walked over to the fence, gently pulled on the wire, and freed the dog. When he returned to the road, his friend said, 'I thought you were the guy who never did anything for anyone but himself.' Henry Ford responded, 'That *was* for me. The dog's cries were hurting me.'

"On the one hand, this is an extreme example of selfishness, where a person can become so self-centered that his soul shrivels up like a dried prune. But it also illustrates the Voice Inside. You see, Henry Ford didn't want to help anyone, but he almost couldn't stop himself. He was preprogramed to have mercy. In his inner makeup there was that Voice that said, 'Henry, the poor animal is in pain, go do something.' Even though he prided himself on selfishness, he couldn't quell that Voice Inside. It truly bothered him to hear a creature in pain.

"The remarkable part is that this wasn't something that he trained himself in. It wasn't a sensitivity that he worked on. It wasn't even something that he considered meritorious. It was against his will. Implanted in him at birth was a sensitivity to the pain of others. When he heard those cries, they reached down to his inner core, to that part of the human that only wants to do good, proper, and noble things. And that part of him was touched, that part was bothered; it saw an animal in pain, and said, 'Don't just stand there, do something. That poor animal is suffering.' He didn't ask for that Voice. He might even have spent the better part of his life trying to squelch that Voice, to deaden it, till it didn't bother him. But it was still there. And when that helpless animal yelped in pain, it caused Henry Ford pain, and he had to react to his pain.

"That Voice is part of us. No matter what level a person is on, no matter how far he has sunk, that voice is there, and it cries out to be heard. A person can spend his entire life trying to desensitize himself, focusing only on his own agenda, ignoring everyone else in his relentless pursuit of self-interest, but that voice remains within him. Sometimes it is buried deep, but it is ever present. And it emerges.

"It's an interesting phenomenon among people that good begets good. It's hard to quantify, but if you are driving to work in heavy traffic and someone politely allows you to enter their lane, not only will that act of kindness touch you, but it will surface later in the day. You may forget about the incident, but later in the day, perhaps when a secretary makes a careless mistake, you will be unusually forgiving; or it could happen on the way home that you will allow someone else to get into your lane.

"It's a universal phenomenon that if we are treated with kindness, we tend to repeat an act of kindness. Our inner spark has been touched. That part of us that is noble and good has been ignited and causes us to act in a more noble, more humane manner. For this reason, even the most depraved person will react well to kindness. Even the most barbaric killer still has that spark of humanity within him. And when that part of him experiences true kindness, it is touched and reacts in kind.

"David," I said, "what we call guilt is the manifestation of that Voice Inside, it's that feeling of dissonance that surfaces when I know that what I did wasn't right. I may have desired the gain that would result from a wrong action, but it wasn't right, it wasn't nice, and that Voice Inside keeps reminding me in no uncertain terms. We tend to look at feelings of guilt as negative things that we have to get past and grow beyond. Society tells us: 'Squelch your inhibitions, do your own thing as long as it makes you feel good.'

"But our Creator gave us that Voice Inside as our spiritual radar, our moral compass. When we experience that feeling of discomfort, it is because we were hardwired at birth to do great things and not to live our lives in a self-serving manner. By ignoring those feelings of discomfort, we are relinquishing one of life's greatest teachers, one of the extraordinary tools that we were given to ensure our growth and development. That voice is actually a warning signal that goes off when we, the pinnacle of creation, act in a manner not befitting our station. For man to reach the heights for which he was created, he must heed that Voice Inside.

"Getting myself to the point where I am at peace with that Voice, where that voice and I are in harmony, traveling on the road to self-perfection, is demanding. My Voice Inside demands that I be kind, that I do magnanimous deeds. It actually hungers to help others. It longs to be giving and compassionate, it yearns for real connections to other people — to be concerned about them, to look out for their welfare and well-being. So it is a difficult taskmaster, but a master that drives the human to everything truly great.

"This Voice Inside goes even further — it screams out for meaning. It demands to be involved in significant endeavors, to accomplish, to create, to do things that will have an impact on others, that reach beyond the here and now. This is the part of me that demands a purpose, some higher direction in my life. It is the part of me that hungers for more out of life — more than just working to make a living, more than just getting up in the morning to make money and then spend it.

"My Voice Inside isn't fulfilled by promotions at work, or a large portfolio of stocks and mutual funds. It yearns for something so much more profound, more significant. It is the part of me that can't be satisfied with the mundane activities of life; it needs something much more meaningful. It won't let me rest when I occupy my life with frivolous and passing things. It cries out, 'What am I accomplishing? What contribution am I making? Is this why I was put on this planet?'

"If this part of me isn't fulfilled, I can't enjoy life. All of the beauty, riches, and luxuries that I have become meaningless. If this part of me isn't satisfied, it colors everything that I do, and nothing is much fun, because I remain — at my core, at my inner essence — unfulfilled, empty, thirsting for something that I just don't have.

"Now, David, I am going to share with you something that may haunt you for the rest of your life.

"You can't run from that Voice — you can't hide from it — that Voice is you. It is part of your soul. You can spend the rest of your life trying to run from it, trying to shut it off, but the voice won't stop. You will find no inner peace as long as you are at odds with yourself.

"I can't tell you the number of people whom I counsel who complain of not being fulfilled, of not having a purpose in life. A woman may be a successful business person who controls an empire. She is at the top of her game; her company is highly profitable and growing, yet she comes to me saying she just doesn't see any purpose in it all. She can't find meaning in her life. What makes her feel that way? She is the envy of so many people, yet she will utter these words, 'Why can't I just be happy? I have everything: a great job, a gorgeous home in the suburbs, luxurious vacations. I have it all. Why aren't I happy?'

"She's not happy because there is a Voice Inside that cries out for fulfillment. It cries out for its needs to be met. We have two choices: either listen to that voice, and, in fact, change our lives — or suffer. I am sorry to say that many people choose the latter. And they run — from interests to pursuits, from work to play, from distraction to distraction. Buy a boat, then a yacht. Watch TV, then a movie. Get involved in this project, then that. Anything, anything, as long as they don't have to think, as long as they don't have to stop and answer: 'What am I doing? What is it all about?' People spend their entire life running to fill that void, but it never works. When they come back from Bermuda, when the party is over, that same emptiness is still there.

"David, you must understand this, you must come face-to-face with this one, cold, hard fact: There is nothing here in the material world — no toys, no amount of money, no amount of honor or recognition — that will fill that void. That Voice Inside is too real, it is too deep.

"Why aren't I happy? Why don't I feel fulfilled? That we ask the question is as telling as the answer. It is because we were created for a destiny that is greater than simply making a living and going about this thing we call life. Because of this, I can't be satisfied with just passing time. I need more out of life. Not more money, or luxuries, or cars; rather, more meaning, more substance, more significance. It is that part of me that says, 'I can't believe that God put me on this planet solely to be involved in the insignificant things that I do. There has to be more. There has to be a higher purpose. There has to be some meaning to it all. For heaven's sake what is it?'

"David," I said, "this is one of those life-changing concepts that may take a while to sink in — but when it does, I think it helps us understand so much about human nature and, more importantly, about ourselves. Why don't we stop here, and pick back up next week? Does this time work out for you?"

"Absolutely," David said, as he stood up and walked to the door.

"By the way," I said, "I hope to meet Lisa one day."

"I would like that," David answered.

Chapter Six

LOVING LIFE AND KILLING TIME

We met again the following week.

"David," I said, "one of the things that we humans value above everything else is life. In fact, murder, the taking of a human life, is considered a cardinal sin in almost any moral code. Even in the most primitive societies, life is sacrosanct. A person doesn't need to be schooled in this — we have an inborn sense of the preciousness of a human life.

"To show you what I mean, David, picture in your mind an inner-city hospital emergency room late on a Saturday night. The doctors and nurses are milling around, coffee cups in hand, everyone laid back, until an alert is sounded: CODE BLUE. A person's life is in jeopardy. A man has been shot. The change in atmosphere is gripping; the place comes alive with movement, focus, energy. When the ambulance pulls in, the level of intensity picks up even more. The once-calm nurses are now scurrying like bees, the lounging doctors are now moving in overdrive. Everyone's energy is focused, all attention is turned, the totality of every being is riveted on that patient, now on the edge of life or death.

"Let's analyze what is going on. These are professional medical personnel doing something that they do every day. A man has been wheeled in with gunshot wounds, a man they never met before. A man who, based on the circumstances of the shooting, didn't end up here because he was an innocent bystander. A man who is likely the cause of a lot of trouble to other people. Yet all of this activity, all of this energy and drive, are all focused on saving his life.

"Why? What gets them so worked up? What makes them so electrified? They could be on two hours of sleep, yet they are as energized and focused as they have ever been.

"You see, David, at that moment, it doesn't matter who they are, and it doesn't matter who the patient is. There is one issue, and only one issue: a human life is at stake, a human life that will or will not continue based on what they do. The gravity of the situation is enormous, the severity of the outcome is tremendous, and they all feel it. The doctors, the nurses, the security guard who escorted the patient in, the attendant who filled out the forms — they are all involved and mobilized in this grand, sacred endeavor of saving a human life. No one needs to be reminded, no one needs to be sensitized, it is something that we instinctively feel and understand — the supreme value of human life.

"And yet, I'm not sure that we know why. While all involved intuitively realize the greatness of what they are doing — and therefore do it with great focus and speed — I don't believe that they could all tell you what is so great about it. What is so important about a life? Why is it so precious? Why do we value it so? We may know it in our heart, and yet we don't understand why.

"Think about it: what wouldn't you give up to remain alive? Is there any amount of money that is too much to spend to save your life? Is there any sum to large? And yet, why? What am I doing with my life anyway? Here I am, I value life beyond anything else. My life, other people's lives, the life of a stranger in an emergency room, and yet, I don't even know why. I don't even know what I am supposed to be doing with it. I guess living. What does that mean?

"This is one of those inconsistencies that we human beings are involved in all the time. Here's another example: How many times have you heard the expression 'killing time'? Maybe you were at the airport and you heard the person in line next to you say, 'My plane doesn't take off for three hours, so I have some time to kill.' Or it might have been between semesters in school when you overheard some of the students saying, 'We have a ton of time to kill till next semester.' Or maybe it was a friend of yours who was unemployed, and took up collecting beer bottle caps just to kill time.

"This expression actually tells us a lot about our point of view: we don't value time. At best, we value some of the things we do with it. We certainly value people, things, and maybe even relationships. But time is something to be used for important things. If no important things are here right now, then there is nothing to do with this time that I have on my hands, so I might as well kill it.

"Now, I don't want to get philosophical, but what is life if not time? What is our entire life if not minutes, hours, days, weeks, months, years? We are on the face of this planet for a finite amount of time, and the ultimate measure of life is time. If we were very pragmatic about it, we might even refer to life as 'how much time I have left.' I am now thirty-eight, my mother lived to be sixty-eight, my father to ninety-two — where does that leave me? Meaning, how much time do I have left to live? I can't think of any clearer and more obvious statement to make than this: **time is life**. And yet, we flippantly speak about killing time, knowing full well that the very essence of what I so value, this thing called life, is only a limited amount of time.

"Now, David, I want you to imagine for a moment that this very same fellow, who when unemployed talked about killing months of time collecting beer bottle caps, is diagnosed with lung cancer. He is now in a battle for his life. The prognosis is grim. He reaches deep down inside himself and makes that monumental decision to fight. Whatever it takes, whatever pain he has to go through, he will do it. He has the emotional strength and determination to lick this thing. And fight he does: he goes through months of treatments that leave him feeling worse off than the disease itself did, he spends days so weak that all he can do is lay in bed and blankly stare, he lives through four months of hell on this earth. Finally, he gets back the report: remission. They got it all! He will live!

"Let us imagine him the day that he is released from the hospital — a man with a new lease on life. A man who only a few weeks ago didn't know whether he would be here at all. He now sets out and plans his future. Can we assume that we are going to see the same person? Can we assume that his view of life is going to be the same as before he got sick?

"On his first walk out onto the hospital grounds, he is on a high. The birds are singing, the first smells of spring are in the air. The gentle humming coming from the fields, the forming of buds, and the fullness of the aromas that surround him all fill him with an inner joy that he never experienced before; it is the sheer pleasure of being alive. Can we imagine a greater sense of supreme well-being? Can we imagine a richer person? Simple bread tastes like a king's feast. Such a man is exalted, with his body on the ground and his mind among the angels. Such bliss.

"But now what? He now has a fabulous appreciation of the value of life. In the core of his being, he understands the opportunity of actually waking up in the morning feeling energetic and well. But now what should he do? Now that he has a new lease on life, now that he can really value each moment and is ready to live life to its fullest, for what should he use this priceless commodity called life?

"You see, we are all in this dilemma. We all have this very deeply rooted sense of the value of life, and yet we spend most of our life asleep to this ultimate question: what should I be doing with this priceless commodity called life? What happens when I wake up? What happens when I come out of my slumber and come face-to-face with that reality that life is precious beyond words but I just don't know why? What happens when I understand in the depth of my being that time is the most precious, limited resource on the face of this planet but I just don't have a clue as to why?

"And so we go on in this complete state of contradiction, all the while talking about the value of life, and yet so flippantly talking about killing time. We love life and we kill time, yet life is nothing but time!

"I want to share with you a story that is possibly the greatest one I've heard about the sanctity of time. When Rabbi Avraham Grodzinski — one of the eminent Torah leaders in prewar Europe — was hospitalized during the Nazi occupation, his students came to impart grave news. They had gotten word that the Nazis were about to burn down the hospital, and they urged their beloved mentor to leave immediately. He thought for a moment and then said, 'I am too ill to be transported, and without ongoing intensive medical care I will not survive. Evacuate whoever you can, and then move me to the top floor.'

"His students couldn't argue with their revered teacher because they realized that he knew his condition better than they did. However, they tearfully asked, 'What good will it do to move you further up?' Rabbi Grodzinski replied, 'When they burn the building, fire will reach the top floor last, so I will have a few more minutes of life.'

"David, when I heard that story, I was humbled. The man's respect for the sanctity and value of life is a lesson worth heeding. Rabbi Grodzinski had the utmost appreciation of even a few additional minutes of time on this world. But time for what? When I see life as precious, I understand that there must be great purpose to it. I know it instinctively, in the deepest recesses of my heart. But why? I realize that my life, which I value to the utmost, consists of time. But time to do what?

"This is the dilemma that confounds all of us: we intuitively recognize the value of life, yet we not only speak about killing time, we actually kill time all too often. We value human life beyond anything else, yet we don't know why. There is something missing here!

"Obviously, David, something bigger than what we have been discussing until now is going on here. Something far more significant and important. There is part of the equation that we haven't yet discussed."

I thought for a moment and then turned to David and said, "Do you mind if we take a break now?"

"Rabbi, do you mean you're going to leave me in suspense until next week?"

"Actually, David," I said, "I think that I've left you with important food for thought. So why don't we continue this conversation the next time we meet?"

Chapter Seven

GOD BLEW IT

"David," I said, "I would like to make an observation: if we look at the world around us, there sure does seem to be a lot of senseless suffering and pain. So many bad things seem to happen: people get sick and die; businesses go bankrupt; there are earthquakes, tornadoes, and car crashes; people break legs and lose hands. There is lung cancer and emphysema, diabetes and shingles, and hunger and famine in the world. There are broken homes and divorce. There are earthquakes, floods, and hurricanes. There is war. It sure does seem like there is a lot of meaningless suffering in the world.

"The worst part is that it all seems so arbitrary. All of the catastrophes that we read about strike without rhyme or reason. A young man, on the way to his wedding, is hit by a truck and instantly dies; a twelve-year-old girl is burned to death when the boiler blows up in the basement; a six-year-old contracts leukemia. And we ask, 'Why?' Why do these things have to happen?

Why all the needless suffering? If pain and suffering were meted out to the wicked only, we might understand it. But it happens to good people, to regular people, to people who are just like you and me. The question is, Why? Why would a kind and just God allow these things to happen? Why would a loving God sit back while so much evil is perpetrated?

"Before we attempt to answer this question, though, I would like to deepen it.

"The Talmud discusses the order of creation:

- First God created matter, the very building blocks of creation.
- Then darkness and light.
- Next the heavens and earth.
- Then the planets and stars, the fish, the birds, and the animals.
- Then, on the final day, at almost the last moment of creation, God made man.

"The reason God waited till the rest of creation was complete before bringing forth man is because the purpose of creation is man. This is much like when one invites a guest. First the host prepares the meal, sets the table, and arranges the settings. Only when all has been prepared is it appropriate for the guest to be welcomed in. So too was it with man. The entire world and all that it contains was created for man. It is his world. So it was only proper that all should be arranged prior to his coming into the world. And so, man was last because he is the purpose and the focus of it all.

"Now, David, that being said, it sure does seem that God blew it."

"God blew it?!" David asked.

"Yes, God blew it. If it is true that God is loving and kind, if it is true that God loves all of his creations, then it sure does seem that God could have done a better job at creating this world, and especially man. In fact, it seems that there is much good in this world that God intentionally held back from man.

"Let's start with the animal kingdom. There are many gifts that animals enjoy that man doesn't. If, in fact, man is the highest order of creation, wouldn't it make sense to take all of the strengths of the animal kingdom and invest them in man? Yet that isn't what we see.

"To give you an example: George Dillman is a karate master. He is also a bit of a showman. He once decided he was going to put on the ultimate karate demonstration. He had already gone through the whole gamut of breaking things: first boards, then bricks, and then large blocks of ice. Now he was looking to do something really spectacular. He decided that he was going to fight a bear.

"Of course, it was only going to be a show, so he hired a circus bear for the performance. The bear had been trained to wrestle, and George got together with the bear's trainer to choreograph a fight scene between "man and beast." Here, however, was the problem. While George may have been a highly proficient martial artist, he had a flaw: he took himself seriously — maybe a tad too seriously. He decided that he was going to make headlines. Instead of just going through the fight scene as planned, he was going to actually knock the bear out.

"On the day of the demonstration, the crowd gathers and George takes the stage. The trainer brings out the bear. The two square off, and the "battle" begins. The bear moves forward, and George steps back. The bear lunges toward him, and George sidesteps. Then the bear swings wide, George ducks, and then he hauls off and smashes the bear full force in the chest. You could hear the thud three rows back.

"Needless to say, George didn't knock the bear out. But he did manage to get the bear angry. Real angry. So angry that if it weren't for the bear's trainer somehow stepping in and calming the animal down, George would have been killed.

George learned an important lesson that day: you can be a high-ranking karate master with twenty years of combat experience, but you can't fight a bear. A bear is six hundred pounds of solid muscle! A bear is simply much stronger than a man.

"Why didn't Hashem create us like bears? Why didn't Hashem make man big and strong and made out of six hundred pounds of solid muscle? Wouldn't it have prevented an awful lot of suffering over the years? Wouldn't man's stay on this planet have been more pleasant?

"Have you ever waited for a bus on a freezing February morning and no matter how many layers of clothing you had on, you were still shivering to the bone? You won't find that happening to a polar bear. Polar bears have a layer of fat under their skin that keeps them warm. In the middle of winter, they break open the arctic ice and go in for a nice dip. Then they come out and sun themselves in the minus-twenty-degree air. Why didn't Hashem make us that way? Why not create us just like a polar bear, big and strong with a thick fur coat so that we shouldn't suffer from the cold?

"Because such a creature might be warm, but he wouldn't be a man," David responded. "He would be just a different type of animal."

"Not necessarily," I said. "I mean, take the same essence of man — the same personality, the same intelligence, all of the features of man — and put him into a stronger, more powerful body. Why not? Wouldn't man have been better off with such a change?

"Let me give you another example. Have you ever found yourself in the dentist's chair in excruciating pain? The next time you do, I want you to think of the shark. Why the shark? Because that mighty hunter of the sea has up to twenty-five rows of teeth, one set behind the next. If one tooth gets damaged, another one falls into place. A shark is born with a lifetime's supply of teeth. Now, wouldn't it have been more convenient to create man that way, with many rows of teeth? If one goes bad, just pop it out, and in comes the next one.

"Why didn't God create us that way?

"It seems that there are many advantages that creatures of the wild have that man was *not* given. He was created as is: weak, susceptible to attack, and subject to the elements. It almost appears as if man was purposely created in this independent-yet-dependent mode, as if he was to be the master of his fate, yet still fragile and vulnerable. And the question that begs to be asked is why? Why not make him big and strong and indestructible?

"An even clearer example of this is disease and illness. Our Creator fashioned a stupefying immune system in man — ready to pounce on every imaginable germ — yet He left huge, gaping holes in that defense system. Take man, the powerful controller of his own destiny. Along comes one lone cancer cell, and our man is no more.

"Michael Zasloff, a biochemist with the National Institute of Health, made a fantastic discovery. While working with the African clawed frog, he noticed that it never suffered infections. Even when researchers performed surgery on these frogs and returned them to murky, bacteria-filled waters, they remained free from disease. Two months after making his observation, Zasloff discovered *why*. It seems that the frog's skin secretes a family of antibodies that protect it from infection. When the frog feels threatened, it emits a white fluid that kills all known forms of bacteria.

"Isn't that amazing — a frog that can't get an infection? A small, insignificant creature that is impervious to disease. How many people have died of infection over the millennia? Before penicillin, it was probably the greatest killer on the face of this planet. And even now, don't we suffer from all types of infections and illnesses?

"Why not put these same antibodies in man? We see that Hashem is capable of creating an organism that is completely protected from disease; He did it for the little frog. Wouldn't it have been kind to give this to man as well? Wouldn't man's stay on this planet be improved? Wouldn't he live longer and enjoy life more without the constant threat of sickness looming over his head?

"If you were to tell me that Hashem wasn't wise enough to figure out all of the answers to man's problems, it would be one thing. But we see a world replete with His wisdom. We see these very wonders in abundance in the natural world. Yet man was given some advantages and not others. Doesn't it make you wonder?

"David, here's something even more interesting. Scientists are now able to identify and measure the effects that certain chemicals have on our moods. When I am happy, my brain undergoes a chemical change. These chemicals are released in different ways. One is by taking medication; another is simply through engaging in exercise. After a sustained period of physical activity, the brain starts to release these chemicals, and the thalamus — the part of the brain that relays sensory inputs — reacts by bringing about a sensation of mild euphoria. Athletes are well aware of this — they call it runner's high.

"Now, I want to ask you a very simple question: We are repeatedly told that Hashem is far more merciful than anyone we could ever imagine. We are taught that Hashem loves mankind as a father loves his children. So couldn't Hashem, in His infinite wisdom and kindness, simply have given us all a larger gland that would constantly release this joy activator so we would be forever happy?

"Why not? It makes no difference to Him. He creates the gland in every embryo anyway, why not just make it a little bigger, and put an end to so much misery in the world. Imagine waking up in the morning, stretching out your arms, and — bingo! — that gland secretes a nice big dose of joy.

"Wow! How great it would be to be alive with just this one tiny improvement! You sit down to a glass of orange juice, and another wave of euphoria comes over you. Wowww!

"Why not? Why not create man that way? It's clear that God has the capacity to do it. With this increased level of chemicals in the brain, man would truly be able to live a life of pleasure and comfort. So why not give it to him?

"And while we're asking questions about man, why don't we ask about pain? Did you ever get a headache that wouldn't go away no matter how hard you tried to lessen it? What good does that do us? How much can we actually accomplish with a migraine? Why have them? In fact, why create pain at all? Granted, some pain is important as a warning system — it keeps us from harm — but there are many situations where pain doesn't serve a productive role at all. Have you ever known someone in chronic pain, the type of pain that prevents them from functioning, that doesn't allow them to do anything other than focus on ways of alleviating the debilitating anguish that consumes them? What possible benefit is there in that pain? Why create it? And if it was created, why not provide some kind of shut-off mechanism? In a system as complex and sophisticated as the one hundred billion cells that make up the human central nervous system, I am sure that Hashem could have installed a timer that would stop the transmission of pain after, say, five minutes.

"To illustrate how strong this question is, let's say that I was given the opportunity to design man. Let's imagine that I were given the chance to take all of the wonders that we see in this world and was allowed to put them together to make man. At the risk of sounding irreverent, I think I would do a much better job than God did. I think that I could put together man in a way that he would be much better suited for life in the real world.

"Imagine a booming voice comes from Heaven and says: 'RABBI!'
"'Yes...'
"'I HEAR THAT YOU HAVE MANY COMPLAINTS ABOUT THE WAY I DESIGNED THINGS.'
"'Ahhh... No, Sir, not complaints. I was just wondering out loud...'
"'IF YOU THINK THAT YOU CAN DO BETTER, THEN GO AHEAD! YOU CREATE MAN!'

"And so I set out to create man, using only features that I find already in this world; I get to pick and choose as I put together a new version of man.

"Wow, what a man I would make! I wouldn't create a puny, weak, poor-excuse-of-a-man. My man would be as strong and indestructible as a bear. He would be as fast as a cheetah, and as brave as a lion. I would give him teeth like a shark, an immune system like the African clawed frog. He would have super-sensitive hearing like a bat, and he would be able to go for weeks without water like a camel. He wouldn't have a problem with pain, not my man — I would give him an automatic shut-off switch. But more than that, he would have a joy gland as large as a coconut. With a constant supply of joy, he would be as happy as a lark all day long.

"Oh, another thing — laziness. Not in my man. I would give him the energy level of an ant so he could work all day without tiring — only at night would he stop to rest, for just a short time.

"Anger? Nope. I don't think that would do him any good; I would get rid of that part altogether. What about competition and jealousy? Not a chance, too many people have been killed over the millennia because of those traits. Arrogance? No way. He would be humble and sweet as sugar.

"What a man he would be!"

David looked at me, laughed, and said, "You are right, Rabbi, that does sound a bit irreverent."

"David, I'm not posing this question for the sake of being disrespectful, but to bring home a key point: It's clear that Hashem is capable of creating all of these features, since he placed them in other species. So why didn't He mix and match them, take the best of each, and then blend them together to form the pinnacle of creation — man? It seems that so much wisdom went into purposely making man exactly as he is: strong, yet fragile; independent, yet utterly dependent; master of the earth, yet contingent upon it for his very survival.

"The key question is: What does Hashem expect of man? Man, who has the capacity to find joy and also to suffer; man, who lives with the full gamut of human weaknesses that entrap generation after generation, so often ending in war and destruction. Man, who is this unique conglomeration of strength and weakness...why create him with this fine balance?

"David, I think we are ready to address that one major question: Why did Hashem create humans? What did He have in mind when He created man and placed him on this planet? But before I offer you my thoughts, I would like you to think about this question. I would like you to think about man and his place in the world we live in. And when we meet next week, I would like to hear your answer to this question."

Chapter Eight

WHAT AM I DOING HERE?

hen David came back the next week, I asked him what he had
come up with.

"Rabbi," he said, "while I certainly spent a good deal of time
thinking about our discussion, I can't say that I have the single
answer to this question. I mean, can man ever really know the one
answer to that question?"

"David," I said, "if we accept that God created man, then, perforce,
we accept that there has to be a purpose in that creation. It would
seem incredible, then, that God would form man for a particular
reason and not let him know what that reason is. It would be like
sending a man on a seventy-year mission, but never telling him
what the mission is.

"I wanted you to spend time thinking about this question because
I want you to feel the profound significance of it. Forget philosophy, forget religion — one simple, vital question that absolutely
demands being asked: What am I doing here? What is my purpose

in life? Can I live without knowing the answer to this question? Can a thinking person really go through life without at least asking this question? What relevance does everything else that I do have if I can't even answer this one essential question? And even more, what meaning can my life really have if I can't answer it?"

"Well..." David said, "I always kind of thought that we were put here to do good, to contribute, to leave the world a better place than we found it."

"In what sense?"

"I see myself contributing to the world around me. Each person has to find his own way. For one it might be helping the poor and downtrodden; another might find herself involved with orphanages and hospitals, or finding a cure for cancer — taking the world from an imperfect state and bringing it one step closer to being a perfect world. While I can't say that I've discovered my particular mission in life, I am always looking for ways to help others."

"David, what you are saying is certainly noble, but it only deepens the question. If we accept that God is omnipotent, He can do exactly as He pleases. So all of the needs that you are going to spend your lifetime meeting, and all of the bad that you are going to rectify, could have easily been done away with from the start. God is quite capable of creating a world where there is no need to work — where your nourishment would grow on trees. God is quite capable of creating man without evil desires, so that there would be no wrong to make right. God could have created a world where there was no war, no crime, and no pain. And as we discussed earlier, God, Who designed the African clawed frog to be impervious to disease, could just as easily have given that feature to man. And, even more pointedly, God didn't have to create this thing called illness in the first place. The point is that God doesn't need help creating a perfect world."

"But then," David asked, "what would be left for man?"

"Nothing."

"So what would man do?"

"I don't know; let him pick ripe fruit from the trees."

"But what kind of life would that be?"

"Much the same as it is now."

"But he would be bored. He would have nothing to do."

"So, you mean to tell me that this world in all its complexity exists just so man shouldn't be bored?"

"Well no, but..."

"But what?"

"There has to be a purpose."

"Oh, David, I sure do agree with you on that. The only question is, what is the purpose?"

"OK, Rabbi, you got me curious. I am ready. Tell me, what is our purpose on this earth?"

"Sure, David, but before I deal with the answer, I need to ask you one more question. Is that OK?"

"Go ahead, I'm getting used to being confused."

"David," I said, "I don't mean to be funny, but — who are you?"

Chapter Nine

WHO ARE YOU?

"Who am I?"

"Yes, who are you?"

"I'm not sure I know what you mean." David responded. "I'm a thirty-two-year-old lawyer."

I looked at David and said, "I don't want to sound like a lawyer myself, but my question was, Who are you? not, What do you do for a living?"

I explained to him that this is quite a sore subject with me, this phenomenon of our work being our criteria of self-definition, where "what I do for a living" becomes "who I am." I can't tell you how many times I have heard that routine, where the questioner asks, "Who are you?" and the person answers, "I am a lawyer, a doctor, or an Indian chief." I find this is far more than a figure of speech. For many people, what they do for a living is the very force that shapes their existence. It is how they approach life, how they look at themselves, and how they position themselves in the world. It goes so far as to become the very definition of who they are.

"David," I said, "do you mind if I share with you one of my pet peeves?"

"Please, go ahead."

"As the years go by, I have officiated at many funerals — far more than I wished to have been at. To me, one of the most troubling parts is when people get up to speak about the deceased. This is the moment to sum up the person, to put forth in a few sentences the full contribution that this person has made — to his family, to those he affected, to the world at large. I can't describe the emotions I feel when someone gets up onto the podium and says, 'What a good provider he was.' As if that is the entire contribution this person has made to the world. He made money.

"Now, don't get me wrong, one of the roles of a person is to provide for his family's needs. As people, we do a lot of things — some significant, and some less so. Earning a living and support-ing a family is a serious issue. But is that the sum of the person? Is that what you would use as the defining criteria of the man? He was a lawyer, an accountant, a stock broker. Should we put that on his tombstone? I know some people do. But isn't that sad? A lion hunts, a cow grazes, and man works. So he is an extension of the animal kingdom, just another one of the inhabitants of this planet, trying to feed himself. There's got to be more to life than that. There has to be some higher purpose, some greater meaning than just going to work each day, making money, then spending it, then getting up again, making more money, then spending that too — and then we die.

"What makes this even sadder is when you take the height of creation — **man** — and reduce him to a thing, whether it be a job, a profession, or a career. You lower the person by limiting him to one dimension. Is this man, for whom the Bible tells us it was fit to create an entire world? Is this man, whom we are taught can reach spiritual heights greater then angels? This is a beaver, busy at his dam; a worker bee gathering in pollen; an ant bringing in some prize to the nest. You have eliminated all of the 'greatness of man.' What about relationships, family, friends? What about kindness? What about making a contribution to others? What happened to helping, to being committed to a cause, to life beyond the workplace? How much different is this than enslaving a human, shackling him to a functional role, like a beast of burden? You exist to work, to do your mundane labor, toil at your task, go through the grind, and then go home to rest up for another day of chores. There's got to be more to life than this.

"So, David, let me restate the question. I know that you are six foot two, weigh 185 pounds, you are handsome, and have brown hair. I certainly recognize that, and I also know that you were born with certain talents and strengths. You are an intelligent, articulate, personable young man. But I want you to stretch, to reach out beyond today, beyond all that you are currently involved with; past your career, past getting married and one day raising a family. I want you to reach deep into your essence and ask a deep, fundamental question: Who am I?"

"Rabbi, I'm not sure I know what you mean by, 'Who am I?' If you mean my spirit, my essence, I guess you could say I am a composite of life experiences and upbringing, a certain level of education, intelligence, and personality. I have a way of thinking because of the way I was brought up. I feel passionate about certain issues based on my values and beliefs. I approach life in a particular way as a result of my outlook and temperament."

By the look on David's face I could tell that I had only widened the gap between us. "OK," I said, "I want you to try something for me. It may be unpleasant, but I think that it will help bring out this point.

"Let's imagine for a moment that you are in a car accident, a terribly tragic collision, and you lose both of your legs. You wake up in a hospital room and realize that you will spend the rest of your life in a wheelchair. Are you still alive? If your physical condition changes so radically that everything you've done up until now has to be rethought, reexamined, and you now have to change your entire life, are you, David Goldstein, still alive?"

"Yes, of course. I would be living a different lifestyle, but yes, I would still be alive," David answered.

"OK," I continued, "let's take this one step further. In this horrific accident, not only do you lose your legs, but you lose both of your arms as well. Imagine that you are a quadriplegic. Are you, still alive?"

"Well, I have to imagine that life would be extremely difficult," David said as he lapsed into thought. After a while he added, "But, yes, I would still be alive."

I looked across to David and said, "I recently read a book called *The Diving Bell and the Butterfly*, written by a French author who had been the editor of a highly respected magazine in Paris. He was in a tragic car accident that left him paralyzed. He describes waking up after being in a coma for three days, only to find that he had no control over his body. He couldn't move his arms or legs. He couldn't sit up. He couldn't even move his head. The only part of his body that he had any control over was his left eyelid — he could blink.

"The book is a chronicle of his time in that state — the ups, the downs, his daily struggles and travails. He explains that his condition is called 'locked-in syndrome' because the victim is locked into his or her own body.

"He recounts that he gave each nurse a name, based on the care or gruffness they show him. Some were angels of mercy, some were mere robots, and one he named 'Attila the Hun.' Throughout the book the reader gets to understand his emotional highs and lows. He tells of the mixed feeling of extreme joy and pain when his children came to visit. He so enjoyed seeing them and watching them frolic, yet was so pained that he was not able to hold them and run his fingers through their hair.

"Interestingly, his is one of the first known cases where the patient was left with some ability to communicate — he could signal with his eye. A speech therapist devised a system for him to express his thoughts. She would hold up a card with the alphabet on it. She would move her finger slowly down the card, and when she got to a letter that he wanted to signal, he would blink. In this manner, he could share his needs and thoughts with those around him.

"Was he alive? When he was in this state, locked in, cut off from the world, was he, the person, still alive?"

David sat lost in thought for a while. By the look on his face, I could see that he understood where I was going with this. "Yes, Rabbi," he responded. "He was alive."

"David," I said, "do you know how alive he was? He was so alive during this period of his life, that he wrote a book. That entire book, which became a best seller in France and was later translated into English, was written by a man whose only method of communication was by blinking his eye. In the mornings he would compose the sentences and paragraphs in his mind, and then, in the afternoon, his secretary would stand at the foot of his bed, taking dictation for hours — letter by painstaking letter. Is there any greater tribute to his being alive than his book?

"Now, David, I want you to try a mental exercise. Imagine that it is you in that hospital bed. You can't move your legs, your feet, or your hands. You can't speak; you are completely locked in. Yet you are still here. You are thinking, feeling, remembering happy and sad times. People come into your room, and you are glad that they have come. They say things to you, and you wish to respond, but you can't.

"Now, David, let's analyze this. Your body is unusable. Your arms and legs lie there limp; you can't move a muscle. So, in a sense, your body is dead, and yet you are alive. The question is, which part of you is alive?"

"Well, Rabbi, I have to admit that I never thought in those terms. I always thought of my life in the sense of being in my body as I know it, being a fully functional human being. But you are right, I would still be alive. As that fellow who wrote an entire book in this condition proved, I would still be alive. And yet, it seems very difficult to relate to myself being alive in that state. I guess you're getting at the idea that my inner spirit would still be alive."

"It's even simpler than that. YOU are alive. The very same *you* who is sitting in that chair across from me. The very same *you* who feels joy and sadness. The very same *you* who thinks, plans, and aspires. When I talk about you, I mean *you*, who lives inside that body. I don't mean your legs and arms, head and chest — I mean *you*. *You* are not your body. *You* are housed in your body. *You* tell your arms to move. *You* tell your legs to walk. *You* tell them to go faster or slower. It is *you* who controls your body.

"David," I said, "I think we are finally ready for the answer."

Chapter Ten

THE PURPOSE OF IT ALL

reached up to the bookshelf and pulled down a well-worn copy of *The Path of the Just,* an eighteenth-century work by Rabbi Moshe Chaim Luzzatto. I asked David if he had ever heard of this book.

"No, I don't think that I have," he replied.

"Let me introduce this work to you," I said as I handed it to him. "This is considered by many to be one of the greatest volumes on Jewish belief written in the last five hundred years. It is extremely enlightening, profound, and far-reaching, yet it's written in concise and simple terms — a true masterpiece. In his introduction, the author explains that none of the ideas that he presents are his own; rather, he compiled concepts from a wide range of Jewish teachings and arranged them in a readable format. That could be the reason this work is almost universally accepted and admired in the Jewish world.

"I want to read to you the opening few paragraphs." I pulled off my glasses and began reading aloud.

The source of all religious observance is for it to become clear to a person why God placed him in this world, and what is expected from him.

What our Sages have taught us is that man was created to take pleasure from God, and find joy in His presence, for that is the true joy and the greatest pleasure that can be found. The place of experiencing that joy is the World to Come, as that was specifically created for this function. This is what our Sages have taught us: "This world is like a corridor to the World to Come" (Ethics of the Fathers 4:21).

The means that lead man to this goal are the mitzvos (commandments) that God has given us. The place for doing these mitzvos is only in this world.

Therefore, man was placed in this world first, so that via the mediums that are provided for him here he will be able to reach the place that has been prepared for him, which is the World to Come.

I paused, took off my glasses, and said, "David, there it is, set out clearly and succinctly. Hashem created man not for his place in this world, but rather for his place in the World to Come, where he will enjoy the good that he has earned in this world. This world exists for the purpose of allowing man to reach his goal, to grow and perfect himself, and then enjoy that perfection for eternity. To the extent that I use this world to perfect myself, I will enjoy that state for eternity."

David looked thoughtful. He said, "I now understand why you asked me to imagine myself locked into my body without the ability to move. You were doing that to help me visualize my soul without being limited to my body."

"That's correct," I said. "But I find the word 'soul' to be misleading. When people use that word, they tend to think of some other part of them — almost like a distant cousin or an alter ego. As in, 'I'd better not do something sinful because my soul will suffer.' What *The Path of the Just* is teaching us is that after my body dies, it isn't my soul that will live on after me; rather, *I* will live on. *I* will live on and *I* will enjoy the presence of Hashem, to the extent that I refined myself during my existence in this world. *I*...not my soul, not my body, but *I*.

"Let me make this a bit more tangible."

Chapter Eleven

"I" AM NOT MY BODY

"I magine that I were to stand up and start screaming at you, calling you every nasty name in the book. What would you feel?" I asked.

"Assuming that you were serious," David responded, "I would feel pretty bad."

"Exactly. David, that's the point. You said, 'I' would feel bad. Not your arm, not your leg, not your chest, not your nerves and synapses, not your emotions — 'I.'

"'I' feel through my hands and feet, 'I' taste with my tongue, 'I' smell with my nose, but it is *I* who smells, *I* who feels, *I* who tastes. You use your body to bring you these sensations, but it is your *I* that experiences them. Who am *I*? I'm not my legs, chest, head, or even my brain; those are tools that *I* use. They are things that were given to me that *I* control. They bring me input from the physical world, but they aren't *me*. And just as my eyes are tools that I see with, so too my mind is a tool that I think with. They don't define me. *I* am the master of the ship. *I* am the one who occupies my body and controls my destiny.

"When my body dies, *I* will live on enjoying the fruits of my labor on this earth. The point is that it isn't my emotions or my spirit or even my inner soul. It is *I*, the part of me that thinks and feels.

"A cute novel written a number of years ago illustrates this concept. The story line revolves around a professional football player preparing for the upcoming Super Bowl game. To get into shape for the big game, he is riding his bike on a country road, and enters a long, curving tunnel. Unbeknown to him, a car is speeding into the tunnel from the opposite direction, heading directly for him.

"The Angel of Death on duty that day is new on the job. He sees the crash coming and thinks, *Why make him go through the gore and the mess?* So instead of actually waiting for the inevitable crash, he grabs the football player out of his body at the very last moment before the accident, and brings him up to Heaven.

"However, the Angel of Death made a mistake. Any regular person driving his bike through that tunnel would have crashed and been killed. But this man was an athlete with highly trained reactions; he would have veered off at the last minute and not been hit. He should be alive. But it's too late. His body is buried; he's up in Heaven. What do they do now?

"The heavenly court meets and decides they have no choice but to send him back. To do that, they have to find someone whose time is up, and put the football player into that body. The closest they can come up with is a rich tycoon living in an exclusive mansion. So this athlete finds himself in the flabby body of a wealthy snob with an entire staff of butlers and maids at his beck and call. The cute part of the story is how he plans to get his sagging, pampered new body into shape for the Super Bowl that is only weeks away. He has the prim and proper servants run football drills with him on the front lawn of the stately mansion as he practices his passes.

"While this is a charming story, it illustrates a significant concept: that football player found himself occupying a body different from the one he was used to. He opened his eyes and found himself in another life.

"That exact experience happened to every one of us. God hand-selected a life that was the ideal setting to allow us to grow. We were put into this body and told, 'Go live your life!'

"David," I asked, "can you imagine yourself occupying someone else's body? Can you imagine the same essence of you being transported into a different being?"

"Well," he replied, "I never thought in those terms, but, yes, I suppose I could picture myself being in someone else's body, living a totally different life."

"David," I said, "You *do* occupy a body. It happens to be the one that you were born into, but again, it is *you* who lives in that body. *You* are distinct and separate from your arms, legs, and chest. And that is because *you* aren't physical, *you* are spiritual.

"We are so used to confusing our *I* — our true essence — with our body, that it becomes hard to separate them; we have trouble remembering that they are, in fact, separate entities. For that reason, from a scientific perspective, it is difficult to define death. Is it when the heart stops beating? Is it when the brain waves stop? What about a person who is kept on a respirator in a coma for ten years; is that person dead or alive?

"Picture this case. A twenty-year-old woman is in a vegetative coma; she is completely unconscious, yet all her organs are functioning — with help. A respirator keeps her breathing. Various drugs keep her heart beating. Fluids are drained from her blood. So her body parts are now doing what they should be doing. From a medical point of view, there is no reason why this person shouldn't be breathing, yet she isn't. The body lying there seems to be alive. And yet is it? Physiologically it is. There is a pulse, there is blood pressure, all her systems are working. Yet she is dead. But is she?

"I find it ironic that when a ninety-two-year-old woman dies peacefully in her sleep and there is no known medical reason, the health department still requires a "cause of death." What do you write? Congestive heart failure? Respiratory arrest? In a sense, that is what happened, but if you really want to define what happened to her, it is that her spirit — her essence — no longer occupies her body. From a purely medical point of view, the cause of death is 'unknown.'

"When two cars collide at sixty miles an hour, the cause of death is obvious. The body that houses the spirit is so broken that it can no longer host it. But what happens when a five-year-old, perfectly healthy child suddenly dies, and the medical examiner cannot determine a reason? What about when a teenager lies down to sleep and doesn't wake up? There is no discernable reason why the body shouldn't be humming along as healthily as a songbird. Yet the spirit is gone; the *I* is no longer there.

"From a scientific perspective, it is difficult for us to define death because we are applying physical measurements to something that exists in a vastly different dimension. It is like trying to weigh light. It would be foolish to attempt to determine how many pounds a strong beam of light weighs. You can measure its luminosity, but weight is the wrong criteria with which to measure the strength of light. So too you can't use physical instruments to measure the *I*. You can't place the *I* in a beaker, add blue dye, heat it, and see what the reaction will be. You can use a gauge to measure blood pressure. You can run tests on the gas levels in the blood. You can measure breathing efficiency. But what test do you run to determine if the *I*, the essence of the person, is still there? That part isn't physical, so no test can tell us anything about it. The *I* is a different dimension, so any attempt to measure it through physical criteria is bound to fail.

"The point that *The Path of the Just* makes is that when my body dies, *I* will live on forever. Just as weight isn't relevant to light, so too death isn't relevant to the spirit of man.

"Rabbi Yisrael Salanter, in his classic *Letters of Ethics*, describes death as being similar to 'taking off a coat.' The same *I* that is housed within my body will emerge, reach heaven, and live on in that state. The same *I* that now experiences feelings of joy, pain, sorrow, and happiness will step out of this body and continue to experience the full range of human emotions. *I* will experience them, not my alter ego, not my distant cousin, but *I*. The same *I* that is speaking to you right now.

"The sole reason I was put on this planet was to grow. *I* was placed in this body, given this one chance to perfect myself here, and then, in the state that I achieved on Earth, *I* will live on forever. Whatever level of perfection I attained before the death of my physical body, I will enjoy for eternity. In the World to Come, *I* will be deeply pained by my shortcomings and immensely proud of my achievements. This alone is the reason why Hashem created us and put us in this world.

"David, if we fully appreciated the significance of this one point, it would change our entire viewpoint on life and would affect every decision that we make. It would impact our values and beliefs. It would significantly change what we strive for and what we consider important. In short, it would have a profound effect on every aspect of our lives."

Chapter Twelve

PLEASURE WITHOUT A BODY

"Rabbi," David said, "when we first started meeting and I asked you about Lisa and Orthodoxy, I didn't anticipate our discussions going quite this way. I kind of assumed that we would be talking about rituals and traditions. While I am fascinated by all of this, I never thought that it had much to do with Judaism. In any case, I'm starting to get a grip on these ideas, but there is one point that's bothering me.

"I have no trouble dealing with *I* being separate from my body, which seems easy enough to relate to. I can even see myself existing apart from my body. And I guess I can relate to the concept of my *I* living on after my body dies. The one area that I get stuck on is that line that we read in our last session: '...that man was created to take pleasure from God, and find joy in His presence, for that is the true joy and the greatest pleasure that can be found.' I find it difficult to grasp this concept of *enjoying* anything after my body dies. When I think of enjoying something, I keep getting stuck in a physical mode. I think of sitting down to eating a steak and enjoying it. But if I no longer occupy my body, it seems hard to imagine enjoying anything."

"David," I said, "the reason it's difficult for you is because we get so accustomed to life as it is, that it's hard for us to imagine it any other way. It takes a while to relate to enjoying life in a very different modality. Let me try to explain it to you with a metaphor.

"Imagine for a moment that you are in court. It is the biggest case in your life. In fact, the issues being debated are so pivotal to the practice of law that the court proceedings are being recorded. All of the senior partners of your firm are in the courtroom, waiting to see how the case is decided. Yesterday, the judge asked you for a brief outlining the key position in your case. He now resumes court and says in a solemn voice:

"'Mr. Goldstein, I have been a judge now for ten years, and I practiced law for twenty years before that.'

"Your heart is racing; you have no idea where this is going.

"'In all my years on the bench,' he continues, 'I have never read such a well-organized, lucid, and logically compelling brief as the one you presented. Mr. Goldstein. You are to be congratulated.'

"And at that moment the judge and the entire courtroom burst into applause.

"David, what do you think you would feel at that point?"

David chuckled. "I would imagine I'd be one happy guy."

"I'm sure you would be," I agreed. "Likely you would be feeling an intense sense of joy; a feeling that begins somewhere deep within you and starts to spread; an elation so deep and so profound that it transcends time and place. You wouldn't walk out of that courtroom that day—you would float out.

"Yet what part of *you* experienced that? Was it your hands? Your feet? Your head? Was it your chest, or arms? It wasn't any part of your body that felt it. It was *you*. *You* felt pleasure. *You* were ecstatic. This is an example of an *I* pleasure, a completely nonphysical pleasure that the *I* experiences. It is a pleasure that has no connection to your physical state of being and thus isn't dependent upon your body.

"If you think about it, there are many pleasures that *I* experience. Listening to music can be a very moving one. Have you ever come home after a long day at work, kicked off your shoes, cranked up the stereo, and just gotten lost in the music? You may have started off in a pretty lousy mood. You turned on a favorite album, and pretty soon your foot began moving with the beat. Before you knew it, you were humming along. Then you started to move with the music, and by now you were in a different mood. You were floating, up there, flowing with the music.

"That was you enjoying an experience that clearly isn't physical. Not your body, but *you*. Your *I* was experiencing pleasure. There are many things that *I* feel that aren't physical in nature. The full gamut of emotions, from love to hate, from rage to jealousy, are things that *I* feel. *I* feel proud of my accomplishments. *I* feel appreciative of kind gestures from others, and *I* feel hurt by words that people say. It isn't my heart that feels the pain. We may euphemistically use expressions like 'a broken heart,' but what we really mean is that *I* have been hurt. Me.

"Can you remember a time that you were deeply embarrassed? If you will, bring up in your mind's eye a time that you were positively skin-burning embarrassed. Perhaps you said a line that was totally inappropriate, and by the time the words came off your lips, you could already feel a burning sensation spreading. It started in your forehead, then spread down your face. You sensed something hot emanating from within you trying to burn out. As it spread, it seared. And you felt an intense pain.

"It wasn't your heart that was feeling it, it wasn't your chest, it wasn't even your soul, it was *you*. And the feeling was so real that your entire being was enveloped in it; you wished there was a hole you could climb into and never come out of. The point is that feelings aren't dependent on your body. Even if you didn't have legs you would feel the pain; even if your hands were numb you would still cringe — you would still feel that same horrible, sinking feeling because *you* are feeling it. *I* am experiencing something that isn't physical in nature and isn't tied to this world in which we live. These sensations, many enjoyable and some quite painful, are all examples of *I* feeling things that aren't physical.

"That sense of elation you experience when you find out you won the lotto, the emotion you feel when you meet your daughter for the first time in the delivery room, that utter sense of joy and fulfillment, the complete feeling of jubilation — can we even describe such experiences? The heart feels them, or, more accurately, *I* feel them, but they aren't physical. They are inner conditions that are so fine they almost defy definition. But they sure are real, and *I* feel them.

"The point is that when I am separated from my body, I will live on and feel all of those same emotions. I will rejoice in my accomplishments or suffer for my shortcomings. But it is *I* that will feel pain and *I* that will feel pleasure, just as I enjoy these sensations on this earth.

"When we talked about the French editor being locked in his body, didn't he experience the full spectrum of human emotions? If we could be there with him and feel his emotional state when he was informed that his book had been published — that his message had been heard, and his plight was now being shared by millions — could we describe that deep sense of satisfaction?

"If you think about it, any joy that we experience isn't physical. Our body feels pleasure, our soul feels joy. Happiness, satisfaction, and serenity — conditions that we value above everything else in life — have little to do with the body. They don't come to us through our body, and they aren't dependent upon our physical state. Most of what makes us human, those feelings and sensations that separate us from the animal kingdom, isn't physical in nature and doesn't depend upon our body for their existence.

"So when you ask what it means that when I leave my body I will enjoy the work that I have done, we are talking about *I*. *I* will feel joy and pleasure — the same part of me that experiences these emotions in my current state, *me*. And the emotions that I will feel are more intense than anything that I can feel while I am locked in my body here. Here, I am enveloped in a heavy cloak of physicality that doesn't allow me to feel the full depths of emotions. But when I leave this earth and am stripped of that outer cloak, I will intensely feel all of those emotions.

"We are here in this state that we now occupy for a short time. Inside my body, in my temporary existence, *I* live. I have the opportunity to grow and accomplish, to perfect the *I* and then forever enjoy that state of perfection that I reach. I have a few short years here, a chance to make the right choices and grow and perfect myself, and in that state live on for eternity. God custom-designed this world with all of the necessary components to allow us to grow. He created all the opportunities and challenges we need to perfect ourselves so that we can enjoy our exalted state when we leave this earth. But this is much more than a side benefit or tangential result — this is the purpose of creation. This is why God created this world and put man in it. This is why we are here."

David stopped me and said, "Rabbi, the problem is that this seems so far away. In theory, I can relate to the idea of enjoying something in a nonphysical existence. I can even accept that God would create us to allow us to perfect ourselves in this world, and then enjoy that state of perfection in the World to Come. The problem is that we are talking about a basis of morality, as you've said something that will affect my life on a day-to-day basis. These concepts seem too far removed from the world that I live in to change the way that I act or the way I view life."

Chapter Thirteen

HELLO, THIS IS MY FUNERAL

"That is true, David," I responded. "For these concepts to have any effect on your life they must become real. You have to feel them. And that takes a lot of work. By nature, we tend to live in the here and now. We tend to feel that the current state of affairs will last forever, and so these types of thoughts seem very far away. To help bring these ideas closer, I want you to try an exercise:

"I want you to imagine a large, carpeted room with dark drapes on the wall. The lights are muted, the mood is somber. In the front of the room are two candles burning. Gathered are two hundred of your closest friends and relatives, all seated, all listening attentively. All eyes are focused on the front of the room, and there you are, right there in front of everyone — lying in a box. Dead as a doornail.

"It is your funeral.

"You look around the room and see relatives whom you haven't seen in a long time. There's your best friend, Bob — you want to run over and hug him, but you can't. You can't move, you can't speak.

More than anything, you are scared; actually, terrified is a better word. Somewhere in the back of your mind you always knew this moment would come, but not so soon. Not now. *I'm not ready, not yet*, you think.

"There are people gathered whom you haven't seen in years. They're all here: your brother Jonathan, whom you haven't spoken to for over a decade, is sitting in the front row. You want to hug him and tell him that you are so sorry for all of those harsh words you said to each other over the years.

"There's your cousin Marni, whom you grew up with. She looks terrible, she's bawling away. You want to comfort her and tell her it's not so bad. 'Come on, Marni, it happens to all of us.'

"You wonder, *Is this real? Am I here? Is this really happening? I can think; I can see everyone. I know that they are here. I can even hear them. I am conscious. Wait, I must be alive — I can think and hear, I know these people are all here. So how can I be dead? This isn't real.* You hear the speakers say all of those nice things about you, memories of you when you were younger, good things that you did in your lifetime. And you want to scream out, *Stop! This can't be happening. Stop!*

"In this one electrifying moment you come to the realization that life has an end. You understand that you were here on this planet for a few short years. You had a mission and a goal, with a particular function to accomplish, and now it is over.

"You watch as they carry 'you' out. All of your friends gather around the coffin, each one placing their shoulder under it. You hear them say those words, 'He was so young.' 'I can't believe it.' 'What a tragedy.' You watch as the crowd moves out of the funeral home. You see them, their faces ashen, holding on to the casket — your casket. They put 'you' in the back of a hearse. The crowd gets into their cars and follows you to the cemetery.

"They all gather around a dug grave. They lay your casket out. You watch as they gather on each side, grabbing the cloth bands that are holding up your coffin. Slowly, they start to lower 'you' into the ground. And it hits you, at that moment the truth comes crashing through: it's over. My life, all that I knew it to be — all that I came to expect — life itself is over. My life. My life is over! It wasn't supposed to end, not really, certainly not like this.

"And now the real panic begins. *Stop!* You want to scream. *Stop! What are you doing? This isn't real. Stop it. I am alive! What are you doing? Don't put me in there. I won't be able to get out! Stop. How am I going to breathe in there? Stop! Stop! Stop!* But they don't stop. They continue to lower you deeper in. You can no longer see their faces. *Stop. Help! Someone, please make them stop!* Your mind races. A thousand thoughts go by. *This can't possibly be real.* Life. Life itself. What is happening? This can't be. You feel a jolt as the casket hits bottom.

"Someone picks up a shovel, turns the spade part backward, and begins dropping dirt. *What are you doing?* you want to scream. You hear the first dropping of dirt on the casket. *Stop!* Then another. The sound is deafening. This wasn't supposed to happen. *Not to me. Not yet!* The next dropping hits, the sound is even louder. *Isn't anyone going to make them stop?!* Again and again, the dirt drops down and it starts to form a layer. *I am still here, what are you doing, stop it!* But it continues; more dirt, more dirt, until a layer forms, a complete layer covers your casket.

"Then it happens. That one moment that you lived your life running from; that one moment that in the back of your mind, somewhere, somewhere deep inside, you always knew would come. It now happens. You separate. You leave your body behind in the dirt. *You,* the *I* that thinks and feels, departs from your body. A new wave of terror sweeps over you as one thought occupies your entire being: *What comes next?*"

I said, "David, why don't we stop here."

Chapter Fourteen

WYSIWYG: WHAT YOU SEE IS WHAT YOU GET

"Isn't it interesting that we have different faces that we show to people? I have found the same person to be very different around me than when he is in other company. A man might be as sweet as sugar in his dealings in the synagogue, then later I find out from his employees that he is a terror at work. Or, sadly, we see a neighbor whom we knew for years, and only after the divorce do we find out that he was physically abusive to his spouse.

"We spend much effort on hiding our true selves from other people, and if we are skilled we can get away with it for a good while. The reason for this is that you can't see who I really am. You can see my face, my exterior, but what is really going on inside me is hidden from you. I may be thinking all kinds of thoughts in my mind, but my face, my outside, presents a very different picture. What would it be like if you could see me — see me for exactly what I was — with all of my good qualities and my bad as well? What if you could see past the smile that's affixed to my face and see what I was really thinking in my heart? What if you could see me when I was doing a good act, and were shocked to see that the real motivating force wasn't a desire to help people, but a drive for honor?

"Did you ever hear the expression 'People usually have two reasons for doing something: one that sounds good, and the real one'? The truth is that many motives are mixed into our actions. Rarely does it cause me embarrassment, because I can hide my true motives from you. But what if for a moment you could see right into the core of who I am and you saw it all? Could you imagine the embarrassment I would feel?

"To me, one of the most frightening thoughts in life is that when I leave this earth, I will be standing exposed, naked for all to see. *I* will live on long after my body dies, and I will be there exactly as I am here, but without anything to hide behind. You, and everyone else, will see me exactly for who I am. Here, I wear this thick coat of a human body, and it covers me up so you can't see me. But when this coat is peeled away and *I* emerge, you will see me stripped naked of my learned behaviors, unable to hide behind any facades or rationales. Who I am, and what I am, will be clear for all to see. I will be as beautiful as I have made myself, or as ugly as I have shaped myself into being.

"The reason we were put into this world is to mold the *I*. That is the sole reason that God created this world: to give us the ability to change, to fashion ourselves. We don't realize the effect that our actions have on us, but every situation in life that causes us to make a choice is part of the molding process. We are constantly being formed. The *decisions* that I make, the *words* that I say, and the *actions* that I take all have their effect on me. They shape me, mold me, and create me into who I am now, and who I will be for eternity.

"Unfortunately, many times we take the attitude, 'This is who I am, this is my temperament — you can't change a leopard's spots.' We fail to recognize how much of 'who I am' is in my control, and how great the impact of how I live my life is on the essence of who I am.

"How many times have we heard the line, 'I wish I wouldn't lose my temper, but what can I do? That's my nature.' Now, to a certain degree this is true. Each person is born with a different nature. If we were to list all the personality traits — kindness, cruelty, generosity, compassion, humility, arrogance, anger, and jealousy — and then we were to create a ranking system of one to a hundred, with a hundred being perfection, we would find that each person has different natural inclinations in these areas. By natural temperament, Sally might rank a fifty in anger, a thirty in kindness, a thirty in jealousy, and a twenty-five in humility. That is her starting point, her ground zero. What happens during her lifetime is that she will be shaped when she is younger, and as she gets older she takes over the shaping process, so that she is molding herself throughout her life. By the time she is a mature woman, her rating will be very different than it was when she began. Now she might have improved her anger to seventy, her humility to eighty, her generosity to ninety — or perhaps the opposite.

"In each of these areas, we are extremely malleable. Each trait is subject to change. A person can go from being selfish and cruel to being giving and caring. A person might have started life with a fierce temper, and during his lifetime made great strides until the flames of anger largely cooled down; now, he stands in front of you a much-improved person. A man may have started out with a tendency toward arrogance, and by using his life appropriately, he may well have reached the heights of humility.

"And this, David, is the point we miss — all my actions affects me. When I get angry, there are two results that come about. One is that I raise my voice and say words that hurt another person. That alone is consequential. But there is a second effect: I have made a change in myself. I have made a change in my temperament, in my essence. Sometimes the change is slight, sometimes greater, but in either case I have been affected, and my anger will now be stronger. The next time a similar situation arises, it will be easier for me to get angry, and my anger may be deeper and last longer.

"Each character trait is much like a muscle — the more you use it, the stronger it becomes. If a person acts in a kindly manner, again there are two results:

1. She did a good act, which in and of itself has great merit and importance.
2. She has brought about a change in her inner essence. She is now a kinder person. Her *I* has changed.

"Similarly, if a person is bombastic, each time he gets into one of his bragging modes, he is shaping his essence. He is fashioning his ego and making it larger, so he becomes haughtier. And he is therefore a changed person.

"When it comes to physical changes, we are very much attuned to this process. I know that if I go to the gym and follow a prescribed exercise program, my physique will change. If I lift weights, my biceps will increase in size, my chest will become more muscular, my waist will shrink. The change won't be noticeable the first time I come home from the gym, but each workout causes a very slight increase in muscle tissue and a decrease in body fat.

"Changes in personality work the same way: every action affects me. Each decision I make changes me. And in some areas, thoughts can have an even greater effect than actions. With arrogance in particular, more of the damage comes from the thought process than from actions. In our society it is rare that a person can assume a role of 'lording it over someone else,' so the outward manifestations of conceit aren't as common as in earlier generations. Internally, there is plenty of room for this process to flourish. When a person thinks, *Few people are quite as smart as me. I outdid even myself this time*, or, *I am gorgeous, simply gorgeous*, these thoughts cause the very nature of the person to change to one dominated by arrogance.

"However, an important distinction between the example of exercise and personality shaping is that a person spends only a few hours a day in the gym. Even if I am extremely dedicated and my goal is to be in fantastic shape, I might, perhaps, work out five times a week for a few hours at a time. But when it comes to shaping me — molding my personality — this is something I do from the moment I get up in the morning till the moment I go to sleep at night, whether I want to or not. Every situation, every interaction with others, every time I am in a life situation that allows me to choose, my choice has its effect upon me. I think, I speak, I act, all of which molds me into who I am.

"The difficult part is that we are shaping our inner self all day long. If we were to count our interactions with others each day, the number would be in the hundreds. From the moment I get up in the morning till I go back to bed in the evening, I interact with so many different people on so many different levels that it is impossible to even keep track. But in each one of those situations, my thoughts, words, and actions will affect me.

"When we leave this world, we are what we have made ourselves during our lifetime. Who *I* have become during my time on Earth is who I am for eternity.

"A number of years ago, when word processors were first released, they were clunky and cumbersome. If you wanted a word printed in a bold font, you would type <B> before that word. That is what would appear on the screen, and it was a signal to the printer to **bold** that word. If you wanted to underline a word, you would type <U> before it, and that word would be printed with an underline.

"In the late 1980s, technology evolved and WYSIWYG, an acronym for 'What You See is What You Get,' was introduced. Now, when you want to bold a word, you click 'B' on the menu, and the word will appear in bold on the screen. If you want to underline a word, you click 'U' on the menu, and the word will be underlined on the screen. *What you see* on your screen *is what you get* in the printer.

"WYSIWYG is an apt parable for what it will be like when we leave this world. What you see is what you get. Whatever level of perfection I have attained when I depart is how I will be forever.

"If petty jealousy was my weakness, it won't just miraculously disappear from my essence. I made it a part of who I am, and that is who I am forever. If my flaw was a fierce temper, that is something I burned into my essence, and it remains with me even when the cause of my anger no longer exists. When life ends, the person I am is who I will be forever.

"This reality is probably the single greatest life-transforming concept. Knowing this principle takes on great relevance because every interaction with another human being molds me into who I will be forever. Every action, thought, and activity shapes me into who I will be for eternity.

"We care a lot about the way we look. How many times a day do we check the mirror or smooth out our clothes? I know people who won't be caught outside on a bad hair day! Even a stain on our clothing causes us much distress because *I look sloppy. I look disheveled and I am embarrassed.* We take pride, rightfully so, in our appearance.

"Yet all of these 'embarrassments' are external. What about something in my character? What about something that is my very essence? And what if it is ugly? What if all can see it? As I sit with you now, David, you don't see my selfish streak, my temper, or my penchant to procrastinate. It's covered up. You know me based on interactions. Based on your relationship with me, you take a composite shot of all you remember and create an image in your mind of who I am. Sometimes you are accurate, and sometimes you are far off, but even if you know a person very well, you can never get it perfect because you are just guessing at what's going on inside.

"What if you could see the real me? What if you could watch my mind as I think? What if you could peer into the essence of me as I go through all of those thoughts that my mind spins out in nano-seconds? You would have a very different picture of me. Then, you would see the real me.

"In the World to Come, that's what you will see — the real me. That's all that will be left, without any touch-ups, for the good or for the bad. Here, I wear this thick coat of a human body, and it covers me up so you can't see me. But when this coat is peeled away and *I* emerge, you will see me stripped of any cover-up, unable to hide. I will be as beautiful as I have made myself...or as ugly. After the final scene of life is played out, the music stops, the curtain comes down, and — *freeze*. You are what you have become up until that moment, and that is who you will remain forever."

Chapter Fifteen

ACTORS ON THE STAGE

"Rabbi," David said, "a lot of what you have said about our purpose in this world makes sense. I find the concept of life itself as an opportunity for growth motivating and inspiring; it gives such meaning to even the mundane things that we do. Just the thought that every interaction with another person leaves an imprint on me and will show itself in my essence for eternity is a very powerful catalyst for change. The question that keeps bothering me, though, is that the system itself seems unfair."

"What do you mean?" I asked.

"Well," David continued, "on a personal level I can't complain because I feel that I was given a good lot in life. But if I look around I see people who aren't as fortunate as I am. I see people born in poverty, who don't have the opportunities that I was given. I see people born with infirmities and handicaps. There are children who are neglected and abused. How can they possibly be expected to perform on the same level as someone born into a comfortable home, with loving, nurturing parents? If, in fact, God is fully in charge and put us on this planet to grow, there sure does seem to be a lot of inequity in the world. How do you explain why one person is born with tremendous innate talent and the capacity to translate it into great accomplishments, while another is so average? It just doesn't seem that we were all given the same chance to grow."

"Your question is based on assuming that we are ultimately judged by what we have accomplished in this world, as if there were a standard measure against which man is judged. But that isn't why we are here. While it is true that God put us on this planet to grow and accomplish, the measure of the man isn't how much he accomplished as compared to others. There is only one criterion against which man is measured: how much he grew in relation to *his* potential.

"God has custom-designed a set of circumstances for each individual to give him the ultimate setting for his growth and personal perfection. What we are judged by isn't objectively how much we have accomplished but rather what we accomplished as measured by what we were created to do. In other words, how close we came to fulfilling our mission in this life.

"To better understand what I'm saying, David, imagine that a famous actor gets a call from his agent.

"'Listen, Jack, we just got a great offer. Tons of money, an all-cash deal, you get the star role, playing next to the greatest co-stars in the industry. But the best part of it is the plot — it's great. The story line really clicks, it's a guaranteed Oscar. I'm sending the script over this morning. Tell me what you think.'

"After reading the script, the actor calls back his agent. 'Bob, forget it. No deal.'

"'What do you mean?'

"'I mean I won't do it.'

"'Jack, what is it? Is it the story line?'

"'No, the story is fine.'

"'Is it the other actors?'

"'No, they're fine too.'

"'So, Jack, what is it?'

"'Don't you get it? The guy you want me to play is penniless and not too bright. More than that, he's a jerk! I can't stand anyone seeing me that way.'

"'But, Jack, that's only the part you'd be playing. It's not *you*.'

"'Bob, forget it. Playing this part means everyone — the whole world — is going to see me as a down-and-out loser. I can't stand the embarrassment. Don't even ask me again. I'm not doing it.'

"And the actor hangs up the phone.

"Obviously, this conversation never took place. Because any actor, as well as every person in the audience, understands that those people up on the stage are playing their parts. They aren't judged by how wealthy or poor they are in the production. They aren't rated by whether their role portrays a life of success or failure.

"There is one criterion for judging an actor: how well he played his part. If his role to play is that of an idiot savant and he does it convincingly, he will win accolades and praise. If his part is that of the most successful man in the world and he doesn't come across believably, the critics will rip him to shreds. He is there for one purpose — to play his role. He is given a certain backdrop and a certain set of circumstances — the character has this type of personality, is from this type of background, has this level of intelligence — and then he must go out there and play the part.

"This is an apt parable of our life. Each person was given a specific set of circumstances and a particular set of abilities. The backdrop is set in place, and we are handed a role to play. Born into a particular time period, to a particular family, you are given a very exact set of life parameters. You will be this tall, this intelligent, have this much of this talent and that much of that one. Then you're told, 'Go out and live your life!' Ford those streams, cross those rivers, and sail those seas!

"At the end of your days, you will be judged. You won't, however, be compared to me or to anyone else. You will be measured against the most demanding yardstick imaginable — you. Based on your potential, based on your God-given abilities, how much did you achieve?

"Whether you are smarter or richer or more talented than the next person is irrelevant. The only issue is: how much did you accomplish compared to what you were capable of? All of the things that people consider extremely important — money, honor, and talent — are just stage settings. They are props to be used; they allow us to play our part. But in the end, we aren't judged by the part we played. When we leave this earth, they don't ask us, 'How much money did God give you? How smart did God make you?' The questions are far more penetrating and demanding, and the main one is, 'What did you achieve with what you were given?'

"There is no objective standard or single yardstick that everyone is measured against, and the measure of man's success isn't in absolute terms. The system is far more exacting. It is based on your talents and strengths, your abilities and capacities. The only question they ask is, 'How much of your potential did you reach?' Eighty percent? Forty percent? Twenty percent? How much of *you* did you become?

"Our life settings have been chosen for us; we have no input in that process. Smart or intellectually limited, attractive or ordinary, talented or not — these are the backdrops against which we live our lives, the scenery of our 'play.' But they don't define us.

"Just as our external conditions are set, so too is much of our inner makeup. Our temperament has been hardwired into us at birth. Studies show that whether a child is bold or timid, extroverted or shy can be determined at twenty-two months of age.

Naturally, a person can work on himself. He can learn to overcome weaknesses, and change the level of his personality traits. But each individual was given certain predispositions and tendencies at birth, and it's his mission in life to use what he was given to fulfill his role to the fullest.

"One of the great teachers of Judaism, the Vilna Gaon, from the seventeenth century, tells us that the most painful moment in a person's life is after leaving this earth, when he stands before the heavenly tribunal and the court holds up a picture for the person to look at — a picture of a truly exceptional individual, a person of sterling character traits, who shows intelligence, kindliness, and humility — a person of true greatness, who brought outstanding goodness to the world, and changed the very world in which he lived. And they say to the one being judged, 'Why didn't you do what he did?'

"'Me?! Little me? What do you want from me? Was I some kind of genius? Was I some kind of powerful leader of men? How could I have done those types of things?'

"And they answer with a telling and most troubling line: 'That picture is *you*. Not you as you stand here now. Not you as you lived your life. But the you if you had become what you were destined to be. That *is* you, had you accomplished what you were put on this earth for. That *is* you, had you followed the path for which you were born.'

"That moment is the most painful in a person's life. Because at that moment the truth comes crashing through — I understand what I was capable of accomplishing. I clearly see the purpose of life and recognize what I could have achieved in my stay on this planet. And at that one flash point of recognition, I truly understand the greatness of man and what he is capable of doing. However, sadly, by then it is too late. My life is over."

I let David absorb this for a while, and allowed my mind to be drawn toward the delightful sound of children playing in the playground next door. I was pulled back by David's next question.

"How should I put this, Rabbi? I can understand what you're saying about being here to play our role, and being judged by those criteria. And that answers part of my questions, but what about a person born into a poor home, where he or she doesn't have the opportunity of studying at the finest schools. What about a young woman born into a broken home, where there is no proper role model, where life is cheap and meaningless? Is she expected to reach her potential? If in fact we are saying that God places every human being on this planet for the purpose of allowing them the opportunity to grow, it seems that there's a lot of inequality in the settings He has provided."

"You raise a good point, David," I said. "To understand why that is, we have to step away from life as you know it, and try to understand some of the inner workings of the human personality.

"I want you to imagine for a moment that you, instead of being born to your parents, the Goldsteins, living in this part of history, were born to a different family, named the Capones, living in the 1930s. And let's imagine even further that your proud parents named you Alphonse. So there you were, Al Capone, growing up without any positive influences in your life. Everyone you ever knew was bootlegging, hanging out in bars, or taking bets as a bookie. Certainly your nature, your very temperament, was that of an opportunist, and maybe even a little cruel. All you ever experienced from the cradle was that it's a dog-eat-dog world out there. You either kill or get killed.

"David, how do you think you would have turned out?"

David sat back for a moment, and then said, "Well, Rabbi, I think I would have turned out pretty much like that infamous mobster."

"I don't think that's true," I responded. "Even if you were given his exact temperament at birth, I don't assume you would have turned out as he did. Many people were born into worse situations than Al Capone, and they didn't turn to a life of crime. In fact, Al Capone was only one of many siblings, and certainly one of an entire generation of children who grew up in similar circumstances. The vast majority of those kids — and even some of his siblings — blossomed into fine, upstanding, law-abiding citizens.

"Al Capone made himself into who he was; no one else was to blame. It was a process of thousands of small decisions that he made over the course of a lifetime, but he, and he alone, shaped the person that he became.

"You see, David, we make hundreds of choices each day that we live. By the time we are adults, most of our choices are habitual, we no longer *consciously* choose them. We have long ago created patterns of thought and behavior that shape much of what we do. But we are the ones who establish those patterns. We are the ones who made those choices and thereby created the personality that is ours. Once we've set up those patterns they are difficult to break, but there is no one to blame but ourselves.

"It starts with choices that shape our **thoughts**, which shape our **actions**, which shape our **habits**, which finally shape our very **destiny**. But it all begins with a choice.

"This is what the concept of Free Will means. We are free to choose how we will act; free to choose who we will become, and thereby free to shape our eternal destiny.

"David, do you remember our discussion about a person having an inner sense of right and wrong? Every human who ever lived under the sun was given inborn knowledge of what is right and what is wrong. That is the nature of man. It may be true that Al Capone had a stronger inclination to do things that we consider antisocial. It may even be true that his upbringing made it easier for him to fall into the trap of becoming the sociopath that he was, but it was his *choice* whether to listen to that Voice Inside, or give in to his natural tendencies.

"Al Capone wasn't born Al Capone; he shaped himself into that personality. Even Adolph Hitler wasn't born evil. Through a long series of life choices, he shaped his thoughts, which shaped his actions, which shaped his philosophy of life. It all started with choices, and often choices about very small issues

"Let me give you an example from a different perspective. Look out that window," I said, motioning to the long bank of windows on the side of my study.

David looked out to the playground.

"What do you see?" I asked.

"I see little children playing."

"Are they angry?"

"No."

"Do they look displeased with themselves or with life in general?"

"No," David answered. "They look quite happy."

"I think that is true; children on the whole are happy. Not to say they don't have their moments, but usually, healthy children raised in a happy home are happy. One of my fondest memories is of my children as toddlers when they would wake up in the morning. While the rest of the house was still asleep, from their cribs they would greet the new day with sweet, happy sounds. Sometimes they would sing snatches of songs, sometimes they would carry on entire conversations with their dolls or toys. I don't think that I could ever capture such carefree happiness again. Children have such optimism and enthusiasm for life, they so enjoy just being alive.

"Look at the same child ten years later, and you are likely to see a different picture. Gone is much of the vibrancy, gone is much of the zest; frankly, by then much of the love of life is out of them. They don't seem to smile quite as often, and they certainly don't laugh as much. I once read a study that the average young child laughs 114 times a day! By the time they are adults, the number is a fraction of that. What happened?

"What happened was that they changed. Children are very plastic; not only do their minds grow in intelligence and perception, their very nature is being molded as they go through their day. Their very personality is being shaped. How they respond, how they react, how they view life, is taking form. Childhood is a shaping, developing process. Not only in the sense of behavior and attitudes but the very nature, the soul of the child, is taking shape.

"David, I want you to understand that the proper use of Free Will is an ongoing, lifelong process. Children don't have the intelligence or self-control to consciously shape their nature, but as adults we do. And whether we are aware of it or not, we are constantly molding our very personalities. Not only in the areas of enthusiasm for life or happiness but across the full gamut of the human condition. Our arms and legs are fully formed by the time we are adults, but our inner core is constantly subject to growth, which is fueled by the choices we make.

"Unfortunately, we pay little attention to the opportunity we have been granted to earn eternal joy by struggling with difficult choices and making the right ones. Life is an arena full of opportunities to do good or bad, but just as important, opportunities to shape our very nature. Every time I resist a temptation, not only have I won a battle, I have also strengthened myself, and am now the better for it, ready for the next level of temptation or challenge. Ideally, if a person were to win all of the battles of life, he would go from level to level in a constant upward pattern, until after a lifetime of spiritual victories he would reach the ultimate level of perfection. This, in a nutshell, is the purpose of life.

"Unfortunately, we don't always win. We also fail. When we fail, we set ourselves back, create obstacles for our further growth, and we make it that much more difficult to win the next battle. When we win, we set the path for future success.

"Life is complicated, and our challenges come in many different forms. When I finally understand the right way to overcome a given situation, a new one springs up. And, of course, since life is not yet over, this new one has no correlation to the old, so I have to struggle anew. Each of life's circumstances is unique and unrelated to the previous one, and it is up to us to constantly overcome our challenges and perfect ourselves in the process.

"But we are not expected to succeed on our own. Hashem gave us a guidebook to show us the way, a divinely authored work that is a manual of how to perfect ourselves spiritually. Our Creator, Who understands the true inner workings of the human psyche, gifted us with a method that helps people reach spiritual heights. The Torah's written and oral laws are formulas and techniques for improving ourselves, and are our guiding lights for a satisfying life in this world and eternal joy in the World to Come.

"Those who choose to ignore the Torah are often like a raft out at sea, drifting beyond reach with each passing wave and never reaching home port because they don't even know in which direction to sail. The name of the game is human perfection, the stakes are very high, and the prize at the end is eternal bliss. Hashem gave us a program to follow, the greatest system for self-perfection. It is our duty and honor to study the Torah, learn its ways, and then apply them to our lives."

"And if a person wasn't brought up to believe all that you've taught me?"

"Good question," I said. "Let's discuss that next week."

Chapter Sixteen

ANIMAL SOUL/SPIRITUAL SOUL

And God created man in His image…

(Genesis 1:27)

I was about to answer the question David had asked at the end of our last session, but instead he opened our discussion.

"Rabbi," he said, "I must tell you that our sessions are really having an effect on me."

"In what sense?"

"Well, if nothing else, it has gotten to a point where Lisa is jealous. She and I spend a good deal of time discussing the issues that you raise with me, and she keeps mentioning that she feels left out of our discussions."

"Why don't you ask her to join us the next time we meet?" I said. "She is more than welcome. In the meantime, I have something I would like to share with you. I'm sure you have heard this Biblical verse quoted many times: 'And God created man in His image....' Did you ever wonder what that means? Or let me put it this way, have you ever seen a man create a world, or even a sun, for that matter? Have you met a man who has lived for even a thousand years, let alone forever? Or one who can control the winds in the sky, or make it rain?"

"I was sure that expression didn't mean literally 'like God,'" David responded. "I assumed it referred to the godliness in all men."

"Of course, you're right." I said. "But to clarify what I'm getting at, I can recite an entire litany of human behaviors that are far from being God-like. We don't have to look very far to find men whose actions seem more like those of animals. So in what sense does the Bible mean that man is created in the image of God?

"To understand this issue, we need some background as to what makes up the inner essence of all human beings. I would like to read you an excerpt from a book called *Duties of the Heart*. Along with *The Path of the Just*, it rates as a prime source of Jewish thought. Written close to a thousand years ago as a guide to life, it is as applicable and universally accepted now as it ever was. *Duties of the Heart* 3:2 states:

> *Man was created from elements that are very different, whose essence are opposites, and whose very natures are in competition. They are his body and his soul. Within man, God implanted drives and desires that are necessary for the continuation of the human species; these are all of the desires for physical pleasures. They are [present] in man as in all animals. If man makes use of them, he will strengthen his physical standing, and the human race will flourish. In addition to these, God implanted within the human soul strengths, which, if man uses them, will cause him to look down on his position in this world and make him desire to separate from it. This is his spiritual part.*

"Within this short paragraph we have been given the formula of man's nature. When Hashem created man, He joined two diverse elements to form his living soul. These are his spiritual soul (what we call his *neshamah*) and his animal soul. The conscious *I* that thinks and feels is made up of both parts.

"The *neshamah* comes from beneath the throne of Hashem's glory. It is pure and lofty, holy and sublime. All that it wishes for is that which is good, proper, and noble. Because it comes from the upper worlds, it derives no benefit from this world and can't relate to any of its pleasures.

"The other part of man is very different. It is exactly like that of an animal, with all of the passions and desires necessary to keep him alive. This is his animal soul. If we wish to understand man, to make sense of what drives him and relate to what matters to him, then as much as we need to understand the *neshamah*, we need to understand this other part of his soul.

"An animal has a living essence. Just like man, it has a part that isn't physical. It is attracted toward certain types of objects and repelled by others. A dog will form attachments to its master and will even risk its own life to defend him.

"As an example, when I was a *rebbi* in yeshivah, there was a fellow in the high school who had a difficult time going home during those Shabbos weekends when the dorm was closed. When he was a little boy, his father bought him a puppy. He and the dog grew up together, and it became attached to him. When he went away to yeshivah, the separation was very difficult on his dog.

"When this young man went back home every six weeks or so, his dog was very excited to see him, and ran out to greet him. The problem was that in its enthusiasm, it would go into a frenzy and relieve itself all over its master's pants leg! My student was not all that pleased with his pet's loyalty.

"The point is that every animal has a part of it that is vibrant and living, and just like a human soul, this part isn't physical but spiritual. When a dog sleeps, its body lies flat and almost lifeless. When it wakes up, its essence returns. That part of the animal is its inner essence, its animal soul.

"Hashem implanted into the animal soul all of the drives the animal needs for its survival. A cat hunts mice by instinct. A bird eats worms because of an inner urge. It would be difficult to imagine a robin thinking: *Based on my nutritional needs, as well as my capacity to hunt for, capture, and digest such foods, coupled with the general availability of such items, I have surmised that it would be best for me to utilize the worm as my food staple.* Instead, the bird hungers for a worm because it has a natural pull, an inborn inclination, toward optimum food.

"Studies show that when animals raised in captivity are released into the wild, they instinctively hunt for the ideal food source for their species. When let loose, Siberian tigers that were orphaned at birth and nourished with bottled milk begin hunting deer, their natural food source, even though these tigers had never before seen a deer, let alone watched one being hunted down to be eaten. Inborn in them are the tools, the aptitude, and the inclination to capture and consume the types of food that best assures their survival.

"So too with mating. Two bullfrogs don't sit down to discuss their future, with one saying, 'Kermit, I think it's time for us to settle down and raise a family.' Hashem implanted into each animal all of the necessary drives for its survival as an individual, as well as the survival of the species as a whole. Those instincts and hungers are part of its animal soul.

"Man, as well, has an animal soul. There is a part of him that yearns for physical things. He desires to eat, sleep, and procreate. Hashem put into man's animal soul all of the inclinations he needs to stay alive. If he follows these instincts, he will survive, and the species of mankind will continue.

"The animal soul forms a part of me. The *I* that thinks and feels is comprised in part of these instincts and drives. Within me, there is a part that needs to eat. We wouldn't say my body hungers for food — *I* do. The essence of me desires food.

"I am made up of both of these parts: pure spirituality and animal instincts. I have a part of me that is more sublime than the angels, and a part that is as impulsive as any member of the animal kingdom. When a dog feels the need to procreate, there is nothing that stops it; desire rules over the animal. I have that side to me as well. Within me is a set of instincts for physical activities and pursuits. The greatness of the human is that the other part of me, the part that is guided by pure intelligence, can control the animal instincts. It can use those drives and passions properly, channeling them to productive and positive ends.

"These two elements of man are opposites, and they fight for primacy and control. As a result, man is in constant flux. The more he uses either side, the stronger and more influential it becomes. Much like a muscle that becomes stronger with use and atrophies with disuse, if a person uses his spiritual soul to control his animal soul, it becomes stronger, and he becomes elevated. If he gives in to his desires, the animal soul gains command. His desires become more intense and frequent. They demand to be fulfilled more often and with more force — and man becomes controlled by his drives.

"In this regard, man's animal soul is different from what is found in the wild kingdom. An animal's desires are set to a certain intensity at birth. They will fluctuate based on seasons and circumstances, but all within a given range. Man, on the other hand, has less restriction on the intensity of his desires. If he controls his animal instincts, they lessen, so it becomes easier for him to dominate them. He becomes their master. If he allows them to rule, they become stronger and more extreme until they are in total command. Then, man is but a puppet in the hands of his appetites.

"The process of living is a battle between these two forces. Ideally, if a person succeeds completely, his pure spiritual soul will harness his animal soul and use it for the purpose of keeping himself alive. Like a captain steering his ship by the wind, he uses the animal soul and its energy to accomplish his objectives and goals. When he eats, it is for the purpose of maintaining his health so that he can properly perform his mission on this planet. When he procreates, it is for the purpose of bringing children into the world and creating a harmonious, loving marriage. The pleasures that he takes from this world are also for a purpose — so that he should have the peace of mind to pursue the elevated path that will lead to eternal joy.

"By using the animal soul in this manner, not only does he increase the control that his *neshamah* has, he elevates everything that he does. Mundane, physical activities necessary for human survival are elevated into the highest forms of positive acts, and the human functions on the utmost level of spirituality — an angel in the form of a man.

"However, if a person allows his animal desires to prevail and he follows their natural pull without controlling them, they become stronger and eventually rule over him. He is no longer able to make decisions based on wisdom. Rather, like an animal, he is dominated by whims and governed by passions until he loses control of himself, and ultimately even the ability to choose. He becomes more animal-like and less God-like, eventually becoming nothing more than an animal in the shape of a man.

"There is another part of me, the spiritual soul. This is the part of me that is considered greater than the angels. This is the God-like part of me that was implanted in me, as it was in every human being. It, too, hungers for things. It, too, instinctively desires things. However, since this component comes from the upper worlds and was created in such purity and perfection, it has needs that are very different from those of the animal soul. It craves to do that which is noble and right, charitable, generous, and compassionate.

It needs to contribute, and by its very nature it can't be self-serving — it needs to give. This part is holy and pure. It doesn't know how to ask for itself, it's always concerned with doing for others. It wants to help, it feels the pain of others and wishes that it could do something to lighten their load. This is the part of me that is pure goodness, and only wants to do what is proper and elevated in life.

"It is also the component within me that isn't satisfied with the physical, mundane existence that I lead. It screams out for something more meaningful, something deeper and more significant. It is that part of me that deeply needs to do something of consequence and substance — to make a lasting contribution. It is this element that is pure and holy. It is this part of me for which it was worth creating heaven and earth. When Hashem created man, it was this entity that He referred to as the greatness of man.

"David," I said, "do you remember that we spoke about that Voice Inside, that part of us that intuitively knows right from wrong? That voice is this spiritual part of me. What we might call in vague terms a conscience, or a sense of propriety, is the voice of the spiritual soul. All of the higher values that we find intuitive to a person stem from this entity. When we find an instinctive sense of the value of a human life, when we see medical personnel who go to any length to save a patient, it is because they were preprogrammed with this understanding, as all humans are. They were born with this side of their soul that is perfect and understands the value of life.

"When we find successful people with good careers, at the top of their game, who just aren't happy, aren't satisfied, it is because this part of them — their spiritual soul — isn't being nourished.

"This spiritual soul is the Voice Inside that drives me to do 'good' and won't let me rest when I have done something wrong. When it feels I have done something that is improper, it keeps sermonizing, lecturing. And it won't stop. It keeps on and on. And I can't run from it, because it is me.

"This Voice Inside is the height of what we call human, and if man would only listen to that voice, mankind would have long ago reached a state of perfection. We would be living in a utopian society, everyone would only be concerned for the good of others, there would be no greed or avarice, there would only be charity and loving-kindness in the world.

"We humans are preprogrammed for greatness. We have this part of us that is hardwired to do only good, to be great and accomplish grand things on this planet. We are also equipped with a part of us that has no intelligence whatsoever, that only exists as hungers and desires. We were placed on this planet to shape our very selves. As we discussed, each of my character traits is moldable, so this balance within me is constantly being affected by my thoughts, words, and actions. The essence of who I am, and who I will be for eternity, is based on my constant choice of which 'soul' I listen to and allow to come to the fore.

"Because man is a walking, breathing, living contradiction, made up of two drastically different elements, completely opposite in nature, man behaves in a most peculiar manner. On one occasion, he is tolerant and understanding, on the next he is inflexible and short-tempered. One moment he is benevolent and kind, the next he is as mean as vinegar. The strange part is that I am not describing some Dr. Jekyll and Mr. Hyde — I am describing...me! Catch me in the right moment, and I am noble and distinguished. A minute later, and I am a self-centered lout. What happened? How do I make sense of my own behavior?

"We don't spend enough energy watching ourselves and seeing who we really are. We are so accustomed to explaining away our behavior in a favorable light that we lose the ability to honestly appraise ourselves. The reality is that we have two sides to us, and depending on when you catch us — and in what mood we are in — our reactions will vary in the extreme.

"I could be sitting with someone in my study, having an inspiring discussion about the greatness of the human spirit, about elevating our lives — all the finest niceties of human behavior. We might go on for hours on end. Later on, I find out that this man went home, got into a fight with his wife, and began swearing, screaming, and much worse. And I ask myself, 'Is this the same person? Can the same human being who just an hour ago was involved in a discussion about the betterment of the human race then go home and beat his wife?'

"We may use such terms as 'he lost his temper' or 'he got carried away.' And while they are certainly accurate, these living contradictions are indicative of more going on underneath the surface. They are a result of our being formed from these two rival elements. When one side has primacy, we are kind, sweet, and considerate; when the other side takes control — watch out. The same person — different mood, different setting — and we are witnessing diametrically opposed behavior.

"Open any newspaper, and you'll probably read about another auto accident caused by road rage. The Buick cuts off the Chevy. In an act of vengeance, the Chevy chases the Buick for ten miles, finally catching it at an intersection, where it careens into it and injures five people. Is this the act of a reckless teenager who needs to assert his masculinity? As it turns out, the drivers of both cars are over fifty! I just saw a sign on the highway: 'Stop Road Rage, Act Your Age.' How do we explain mature, sophisticated people acting in a manner so unbecoming to their station in life?

"Can you imagine their embarrassment if, when they are about to crash into the other vehicle, they see the driver is someone they know? How about if it's their boss? They would be deadly embarrassed, because they are acting like a ten-year-old throwing a temper tantrum. Yet this is so common that it has become an epidemic on our roads.

"And how do we explain it when driven people, powerful goal-setters who are extremely successful at what they do, throw away everything they have — their career, their marriage, and their reputation — for a bad choice in their personal life? If we claim to understand the very fabric of the human personality, how do we make sense of it?

"The answer is that after giving in to his desires, man loses control. He becomes animal-like, ruled by desires and passions. Animals are governed by instincts. When the desire to mate hits, no controlling agent holds it back. People who have owned a pet in heat will tell you stories of cats jumping through plate glass windows and dogs digging holes under garden fences.

"Man, too, has urges and desires, but he has the capacity to control and harness them. If he does, then those drives, while still a part of him, lessen in intensity and in the urgency with which they demand being fulfilled. When he gives in to these passions without marshalling them, he effectively gives up control over himself. His urges grow and become more demanding, more incessant, and more potent. They begin affecting his judgment and decisions, and exert more and more influence until they ultimately rule over him. Eventually, they develop a master-slave relationship, and he reaches a point where he will do things that are self-destructive, completely against his self-interest.

"Throughout the process, he may think that he maintains control, but like a drug addict who needs a fix, the urge becomes so strong and demanding that it would take superhuman effort to resist it. His desires didn't start that way. At an earlier stage in his life, they didn't envelop him to the extent they do now. It is a long process of 'giving in' that allows these desires to become stronger, causing him to slowly lose more and more control, until he finds himself in a position in which he is almost powerless to stop them.

"The challenge of life is to perfect ourselves by finding the path that brings about our growth and allows our instinctive desire to do what is right and noble to win out. The choices that we make shape the very person we are. The difficult part is that it is *I* who is in contradiction. It is *I* who wants to grow — and the very same *I* who wants to mire in the mud. It is *I* who wishes to shoot for the stars, to reach the heights of humanity — and it is *I* who is satisfied to go on living without a plan, without direction, just taking life as it comes.

"To help man succeed, Hashem gave us a method that allows that part of me that is great to come to the fore. He gave us a program for spiritual development, a system for accomplishing our life's mission. That system is the Torah, the God-given Written and Oral Law bequeathed to the Jewish people on Mount Sinai.

"The Torah provides us with guidelines — and a system of living — that allows all that is great in humankind to flourish. It is the program that allows the spiritual part of man to grow and dominate the 'animal' within him. The Torah is replete with commandments and precepts, many of whose meanings are readily understood, and others that take greater depth to understand. All of these focus on one goal: to strengthen man's spiritual side, to allow it to emerge victorious, and to ultimately gain primacy. Torah life allows that part of me that is great, that part of me that has the potential to be greater than the angels, to shine forth, so I can reach the heights of greatness for which I was predestined.

"David, we've covered a lot. Let's stop here. Please encourage Lisa to join us next week."

Chapter Seventeen

THE PANTS-TOO-SHORT
SYNDROME

When Lisa and David walked in, I couldn't help but notice what a handsome couple they were — both tall, well-dressed, and with such an air of confidence about them.

"Hi! So you must be Lisa," I said. "It's a pleasure to meet you. I've heard so much about you. Please have a seat."

"Thank you," Lisa answered, as she sat down. "David has told me a lot about you as well. It's a little awkward finally meeting you. I feel like a kid standing outside the stadium while the game is going on, listening for the cheering of the crowds and imagining who's winning."

"In what sense?" I asked.

"You and David have been meeting for several months now, and while I get to hear much of the content, it comes to me secondhand; I've never got to actually be a part of the discussions. I feel that much of what you've been speaking about involves areas that I haven't properly explored myself, and to be honest, I've been having trouble with some of the topics."

"Which particular area is troubling you?" I asked.

"I don't know how much David has told you about my background," said Lisa, "but I grew up keeping Shabbat, the holidays, and kosher. I went to a Jewish school, kind of, but the Jewish hours were limited and boring. Despite all the years there, I really don't know as much about Judaism as I should. Overall, to be honest, I found the whole Jewish experience empty — I just didn't feel anything. Even my bat mitzvah didn't feel like a religious experience, it was more like a party. Once I went away for college, I even stopped keeping Shabbat for a while."

"What changed?"

"That's kind of an interesting subject. For me it wasn't like some kind of spiritual awakening or even a philosophical one. It was more of a family thing. It started when I was a junior in college. One of my roommates happened to be a very religious girl. She kept all the things I had stopped keeping, and more. Often, we would get into discussions about the meaning of these things, but her explanations had little impact on me — until she invited me to her house for one Shabbat.

"She would go home every weekend, and her whole family would get together. Shabbat in my house growing up wasn't anything to look forward to — "don't do this" and "don't do that" — a bunch of rules and little joy; so I wasn't really interested in joining her. I turned her down, but she kept asking me, so finally I said yes. What I saw blew me away! She was the oldest of six children. Here they were, her mother, father, grandmother, grandfather, and all the children, sitting around the table, all enjoying it tremendously. During the meal, the discussions were lively, focused, and meaningful; I sensed such a calm unity in how they interacted. This was not the Shabbat I had growing up.

"What struck me more than anything was how the children behaved. They were so respectful — especially the way they interacted with their grandparents. I know this may sound judgmental, but I mean it in a good sense: they actually respected them. It wasn't like some kind of 'let's humor the old folks.' They were really listening and wanted to hear what their elders had to say. I compared this to my own upbringing and realized how different it was. It was very clear that I had missed something growing up.

"I went often to my roommate's house, and pretty soon I began attending shul with her. I met other families, all with the same strong attachment, and before I realized what was happening, I became a part of their community. Slowly but surely, I was keeping Shabbat again. I had adopted a way of life that I saw as so wholesome that I wanted to be a part of it, I wanted to raise my own family that way. The main thing that attracted me was the concept of the family connected through a strong, common bond. I guess you could call me a social Jew."

"That's great," I responded. "There's no question that family plays an essential role in our religion, and the focus of much of what we do revolves around keeping a proper balance in our lives. So what's the problem?"

"Well, it seems to me that many of your discussions with David are based on the premise that all of the mitzvot are vehicles to perfect man, and that the whole reason we were created is to allow us to grow so that for eternity we can enjoy the reward we earned while living in this dimension. In fact, I recall David saying that he learned in this very room that God created us 'not for our place in this world, but rather for our place in the World to Come.' Am I on track, Rabbi?"

"Yes," I said. "I think that's an accurate synopsis of our discussions."

"Rabbi," Lisa said, and then hesitated, as if she was almost afraid to continue.

"It seems as if you have something on your mind," I prompted.

"I do. But I'm not sure that I should be voicing it."

"There's only one way to tell, Lisa. Ask, and we'll find out."

"I mean...I know that we are supposed to have faith, and I certainly appreciate how much time you've spent with David. I'm just not sure whether this issue that's troubling me is something that we need to take on faith."

"Lisa, before you continue sharing your concerns, let me share a story with you. When you say the word 'faith,' I assume you mean a sort of vague uncertainty that will never be cleared up, as if 'belief' and 'faith' mean simply accepting things when you're really not sure. The fact is, Lisa, that that type of faith has little to do with the practice of Judaism.

"Let me explain what I mean. I was once having a discussion with an older woman who had come to synagogue on Rosh Hashanah. When we spoke, she told me that she had found the experience horribly boring. She quickly assured me that she had fasted on Yom Kippur, and had continued going to services even though she saw no meaning in them. In the course of conversation, I mentioned to her that not only do I pray on holidays and Shabbos, but three times each day as well. It was then that she said to me, 'Rabbi, I guess it's just a matter of faith, and I also guess that you have more faith than I do.'

"Lisa, in retrospect I agree with her, it *is* a matter of faith, but it is *she* who has far more faith than I. You see, for me to pray, or to observe the rituals of Judaism, fundamentally makes sense. It is something that fits into a pattern of service of Hashem and an exercise in self-perfection that appeals to me. I understand their effect on me and on the higher spheres, and I relate to them as powerfully constructive and meaningful acts — so it doesn't take much faith for me to do these things. But this woman was continuing to do something that made no sense to her — she continued to go to services on Rosh Hashanah even though to her it was mindless activity, she continued to fast on Yom Kippur even though she didn't see the purpose of it. She did these things for only one reason — because her parents did them before her, and that takes tremendous faith.

"In Judaism, we do very little based on that kind of faith, a word that really translates as 'just accepting things.' Our belief system, and all that we do both in terms of commandments and customs, is based on *knowledge,* not faith. The whole process of studying Torah and becoming more familiar with the mitzvos is one of questioning in order to understand. It takes a while to gain the complete picture — until the significance of everything fits into a larger picture — so we may *begin* by doing things that we don't yet fully fathom, but the basis of it all, and the end goal, is understanding, certainly *not* faith. So, please, go ahead, Lisa, ask whatever is on your mind."

"OK," Lisa said. "Here's my point. I now consider myself a religious person again. For the past number of years, I have been keeping the mitzvot, yet I haven't ever really thought about the topics you've been discussing with David. I agree that the idea of a person needing a purpose in life makes a lot of sense, but it seems that religion would serve a great purpose without philosophical introspection. All of the rituals would still add to our enjoyment of life-cycle milestones; studying Torah would still help us be more moral, better people; and each of the holidays would still have its special message.

"So, Rabbi, how do you know that the theories you discussed with David are right? I don't mean this in a disrespectful manner, but how do you know that your way of looking at life — and our purpose in living on Earth for a set number of years — is correct? And if it is, who says it's necessary?"

"That certainly is a fair question," I answered. "How does any human being — who is here today and gone tomorrow, whose life passes like a puff of smoke — have the audacity to think that he has a worldview that addresses the very essence, the very purpose, of life? That would be sheer arrogance and maybe even stupidity. For that reason, I agree that had our discussions been based on my opinions, my thoughts, and my conclusions, then I would be on shaky ground. After all, how do I know that I am correct? How could I sit down and offer you a course by which to lead your life, when, in fact, it might be dead wrong?

"That's why I want to make one point very clear: what I've been discussing with David isn't *my* personal philosophy. This isn't *my* theology or *my* brand of religion. What we are speaking about is a central part of the Torah — the Written Law and Oral Tradition given by Hashem to Moses and the Jewish nation at Mt. Sinai. These are teachings that were transmitted by our forefathers dating back more than three thousand years, without changes and without deviations. These are eternal words of truth that have been handed down from parent to child, scholar to student, generation to generation, in an unbroken chain of oral transmission, emanating from Hashem Himself.

"This isn't 'The World According to Rabbi X,' to be argued with by Rabbi Y, to be refuted by Rabbi Z. What David and I have been talking about are fundamental tenets of Judaism, all part of the Torah written by Hashem Himself, handed down in an unbroken chain to this very day. And as such it has been taught, studied, reviewed, and passed down to us without changes or modifications as a guide to life and our road map for living."

David looked at me and said, "That's part of the problem, Rabbi. You are saying that the Bible, or the Torah, is our guide to living life now?"

"Exactly."

David looked uncomfortable as he said, "I can't say that I ever articulated this, but in the back of my mind I always looked at the Bible as sort of...well, kind of like a book of stories. I'm sure they are all meaningful and instructive, but in terms of being a guiding light for our lives today... I mean, I find it difficult to see how sto-ries about building an ark or about Moses negotiating with King Pharaoh have much relevance to my life."

"David," I said, "you aren't the first person to raise this point. I often find myself speaking with sophisticated, intelligent people who understand the vastness and complexity of the world in which we live. Together, we may even enter into discussions about the extraordinary wisdom that is manifest in every facet of the world, and we have no problem taking the next step — recognizing that all of this was created by Hashem.

"They fully acknowledge that before creation there was nothing, and that then, with words alone, Hashem created this entire phe-nomenally complex world that we live in. There was no such entity as light, and Hashem said, 'Let there be light,' and light came into being — with all of the power, properties, and intricate laws of quantum physics. There was no such thing as matter, and Hashem said, 'Let there be...' and all of the laws of matter and physics came into being. These highly intelligent people admit that all of the vast wisdom and sheer wonder of this world, which after millennia of discovery man has only begun to scratch the surface of understand-ing, was brought into existence by Hashem with words alone.

"And yet these very same people, who fully appreciate all of the wisdom manifest in creation, view the manual for a meaningful life written by the Creator as a simple book written for primitives, with no real relevance today. As if the Creator, whose wisdom is so clearly visible in everything that He made, set out to write a work contain-ing the secrets of life and couldn't do any better than write a book of simplistic Bible stories. Sort of makes you wonder, doesn't it?

"I have a feeling that the reason people may look at the Torah as a book of simple stories is because they fall prey to what I call the Pants-Too-Short Syndrome. Here's what that means: if you go to a synagogue on a major Jewish holiday, look around at the young men who are almost fourteen years old. You will find at least one of them whose pants legs end somewhere between his ankles and his knees (most often closer to his knees).

"This came about because this young man had his bar mitzvah sometime that year. In honor of the event, he went with his mother to buy a new suit, and they had it tailored until it fit perfectly. After the bar mitzvah, when all the aunts, uncles, cousins, and friends went home, this young man put away his new suit. But now it's six months later, and for an occasion such as Passover (or maybe Rosh Hashanah) it's appropriate for him to wear his bar mitzvah suit. So he pulls it out of the closet and proudly wears it to synagogue. He forgot one point, though: he grew a lot since his bar mitzvah, and the suit no longer fits.

"For many people, this example is comparable to their understanding of Torah. Most Jews had some instruction in Bible when they were young. Maybe they went to Sunday School, but that was it. They haven't been studying Torah since then, so their knowledge of the Bible ended at the comprehension level of a ten- or twelve-year-old. They are now mature adults dealing with real-life issues — questions about the meaning of life, moral dilemmas, and difficult life decisions. What bearing does a fifth-grade understanding of the Torah have on these weighty issues? Since they only possess a childish understanding of Torah, of course it has no relevance to their life as a mature person. It's like putting a child's suit on an adult — it doesn't fit.

"I think this is a large part of the reason that some of our own youth, when searching for spirituality, wander off to other religions. How can they not, when they are unaware of the meaning, depth, and profundity contained in the Torah given to us by Hashem, and how it is relevant today, and to them?

"The only solution for them, and for all Jews who weren't fortunate to be raised to understand the value and profundity of their heritage, is to begin studying Torah as mature adults so they can discover the depth contained within it, as well as its relevance to our lives. Even those who keep many of the mitzvos don't always understand what they're really doing and why. When Hashem gave us the one work He authored, it wasn't only meant for the people of those times — it was given for eternity, to be the guidebook for all people in all generations to come. It was meant to be eternally relevant and eternally fitting, to be as much a force in our lives now as it was three thousand years ago, and as it will be until the end of time.

"Some things change, but the meaning and purpose of life don't. So too, the system Hashem devised for man to lead a happy, prosperous life — and to find fulfillment in this world — doesn't change. This system of living was given by Hashem to man so that he would have the tools with which to achieve perfection. Jews have studied this original Torah — without it having been watered down to fit the norms of current times — for millennia. It is timeless and unchanged, having been so designed by the Master of the Universe, Hashem Himself."

While I took a sip of water, David sat lost in thought, as did Lisa. I had given them much to ponder! Then David said, "Rabbi, I hear your point that the only possible source that one could rely on for the ultimate truth would have to be authored by God — and you say that the Torah is that book. But that brings me to another issue that bothers me. To be honest, until we began our weekly discussions, I never thought of the Bible as having been written by God. I always assumed that the Greeks have their mythology, the Romans have their gods, and Jews have their legends and parables, collected by wise men to aid us in living a more ethical life. How do you know that the Bible was actually written by God?"

Chapter Eighteen

TORAH FROM SINAI

"David," I said, "you certainly raised a valid concern last week; one that will shape the entire course of our future discussions. If your assumption is right, that the Torah is a collection of stories — maybe even a code of ethics — compiled by wise men of previous generations, then while it may rank as a significant piece of literature, we certainly can't give it too much weight. However, if it were written by Hashem himself, then its value is immeasurable."

"I agree," David answered. "But that's the key question, Rabbi — whether, in fact, it was written by God or not."

"OK," I said. "Let's see whether there is any proof that the Torah was authored by Hashem.

"The eleventh century *Kuzari*, one of the great works of Jewish thought, makes an important observation. One of the points that distinguish Judaism from other religions is the claim upon which it is based. Every religion starts with one man claiming to have experienced a dream or a religious experience. It might be backed

120

up by a tight-knit band of his disciples saying they witnessed a miracle, but in the end, it's based on an event that is difficult to substantiate and easy to falsify. Maybe it did occur as we are told, but maybe it didn't; there's no way to know. It may well have been a way to gain support for what one man thought would be a worthwhile spiritual ideal, but we have no way of verifying that the event ever happened.

"Judaism's claim is that an entire nation of more than three million people of all ages heard Hashem speaking to them. An entire huge assemblage heard Hashem telling them the Ten Commandments, instructing them in the basics of Jewish belief. When you think about it, this is a claim that is impossible to falsify and easy to substantiate.

"In Exodus 19:9 and 19:11, the Bible describes the giving of the Torah.

> And God spoke to Moses, saying, 'I will appear to you in the thickness of cloud, so that the nation should hear Me speak to you, and so that they will trust in you forever… Tell the nation to prepare for three days, for on the third day God will appear to the entire nation, on Mt. Sinai.'

"These verses tell us that the entire nation of Israel was gathered at Mt. Sinai when Hashem Himself spoke to them.

"Now, let's think about this. This event happened three months after the Jewish nation had been taken out of bondage. The Torah states that six hundred thousand men between the ages of twenty and sixty left Egypt. Add the women, and we are now dealing with a group of 1.2 million. Add those older than sixty and younger than twenty and you have at least three million people witnessing an event. The claim Judaism makes is that Hashem appeared to the Jewish nation in the most public manner imaginable. The question is: Can something public be falsified?

"David, did you ever hear the expression, 'Ask two Jews, you'll get three opinions'? We are known to be a very opinionated people. From the moment the Torah was given on Mount Sinai until today, we have been a questioning people — we don't merely accept things. The Bible itself calls us 'a stiff-necked (i.e., stubborn) people.'

"The Jewish nation spent forty years in the desert preparing to enter the land of Israel. We tend to have this glorified view that every Jew during that period obeyed the word of Hashem unquestioningly. While it's true that the nation on a whole was on an exalted level, there was quite a bit of dissension, particularly against their leader Moses. Some were jealous of Moses, as he now occupied what they viewed as a throne of glory. He had been chosen to be the one to go up to heaven and bring down the law from Hashem Himself, and he was now the teacher of the nation—certainly enough to engender jealousy in some Jews.

"On a number of occasions, the Torah tells us that groups formed to oppose Moses. When there was no water, there was dissension against Moses. When the people were tired of eating manna, there was opposition. When Hashem told him to appoint his brother, Aaron, as the high priest, Korach and his adherents staged an outright rebellion against Moses.

"Keeping this in mind, I have an observation to make: The Torah and the study of the Torah were central to the Jewish people in the desert; their main activity during the forty years they spent before entering the Land of Israel was studying the Torah. That was a period of spiritual growth for the Jewish People, an interval for increasing knowledge and understanding of the Torah. The custom that we keep to this day of reading the weekly portion of the Torah on Shabbos was begun by Moses himself, in the desert.

"So I have one simple question to ask. Why don't we read that even one person questioned the entire story of the giving of the Torah on Mount Sinai? If there was even the slightest inaccuracy of any sort when they were reading about that event, someone would have gotten up and said, 'Hey, this stuff is a pack of lies! I was there, and it never happened that way.'"

At this point Lisa interjected, "Rabbi, that doesn't prove anything. In fact, what you're using as proof is a prime example of circular logic: If, in fact, the events occurred, and they were read about in the weekly Bible portion from the time the Jews were in the desert until today, then what you are saying is consistent. But how do we know that the entire sequence of events ever happened? Maybe the entire Bible was something that came about centuries later. Maybe a thousand years ago the rabbis introduced the entire episode."

"Good," I said. "To properly answer you we have to fully understand the central role that the Torah has played in our nation's history. To our people the Torah isn't some obscure law book stored away to be read only by scholars. For thousands of years, it has been the foundation of our people. Wherever we went, to whichever country we were exiled, the Torah and its study came with us. From antiquity, we have been known as the People of the Book. Long before there was a printing press, long before books became something found in every person's home, Jews acquired that accolade. Our reputation has always been that of a studious people, and throughout history what we studied was the Torah.

"Every Jewish child began his education with the Torah, and continued this study throughout his life. The same Torah that is read weekly in our synagogues has been read for thirty-three hundred years — read, studied, discussed, and analyzed. The Torah has been the center of Jewish life throughout the ages; it was taught from father to son, mother to daughter, teacher to student in an unending tradition. How does one falsify such a document?

"The Torah has been the most basic theological document for the Jews since we left Egypt. It has been the center of discussions of learning, of lectures, and of scholarly works. It has always been the treasured domain of the scholar and the layman alike. Today, an overwhelming number of Jews attend colleges and universities, but for millennia the sole source of intellectual stimulation for the Jewish people, who were barred from institutions of higher learning, was the study of the Torah. Individuals, families, and communities were involved in its study. For millennia, the mark of the Jewish man and his standing at home and in the community was based on his Torah knowledge and scholarship.

"Over twenty-five hundred years ago, in the time of King Chizkiyahu, there was a survey done in the Land of Israel, and they couldn't find a single school-age child who wasn't fluent in the complex laws of spiritual impurity. In the Middle Ages, the great Maimonides complained about the common people in his time who devoted 'only' three hours a day to Torah study! He wasn't complaining about the scholars, he was writing about simple workers, regular members of the Jewish People, and Maimonides was complaining that they weren't diligent enough in their Torah studies because they only set aside a few hours a day for its pursuit!

"In Eastern Europe before World War II, the simplest craftsmen prided themselves on their knowledge of Torah. Every Jewish community had its house of study. Larger towns had separate study halls divided by profession — there was the tailor's house of study, the shoemaker's house of study, and a separate one for blacksmiths. The Torah was the pride and joy of our nation. In it we found mental stimulation, our heritage, our connection to Hashem. It was a golden heritage that parents gave over to their children. Who could possibly introduce a change in something so central to a people and hope to get away with it?

"What makes the idea of the Torah being written at a later date even less tenable is the very method that is employed in the study of Torah. To illustrate this point, I want to share a personal story with you. After I completed high school, I went to study in Israel for a year. While there I decided to return to America and continue learning in a rabbinical seminary, so when I arrived home I enrolled at one of the major seminaries in New York city, headed by a world-famous Torah sage.

"The first week I was there, the head of the seminary gave a lecture, and afterward some of the senior students were standing around discussing points raised during the class. It sounded like a heated debate, so I walked over to listen. Frankly, it wasn't a discussion, it was more like a battle — they were tearing apart the lecture that we had just listened to: 'How do you know?' 'Maybe it was that way!' 'You have no proof!' Point, counter point. Point, counter point. Jab, duck, jab, duck, counter punch. A number of the students were defending the lecture, others were attacking it; back and forth, back and forth. The speed of the arguments and the power of the reasoning were amazing — it was something I had never experienced to such a degree. For me, it was a seminal point: the study of the Torah, specifically the Talmud, is an extraordinarily intense, rigorous mental process, where nothing is taken for granted.

"The Talmud — which you surely know, Lisa, is the Oral Law given to Moses by Hashem at Sinai along with the Written Law — is all about logic, logic that leaves no room for assumptions, no room for lazy thinking, no room to say, 'Well, it must make sense or the rabbis of the Talmud never would have accepted it.' Rather, it's a most demanding, critically honest procedure of analysis, through the process of questions and answers: 'How do you know?' 'Maybe it was that way!' 'You have no proof!' Questions, questions, questions, and then finally some more questions all focused on arriving at the truth.

"In our Torah study centers, if a senior rabbi is giving a lecture and one of the students is able to posit an argument that threatens the thesis being presented, he is considered one of the rising stars in the yeshivah. Torah study is the ultimate process of questioning and probing in order to descend to the depth of human understanding and discover irrefutable, absolute truth. Those who study Torah are always looking to unearth the hidden meaning, always looking to uncover the thought process behind the position, and always asking questions — nothing is taken on faith, nothing is taken for granted.

"I often wonder what the scene would look like if a Catholic priest were to would walk into one of our rabbinical seminaries, walk to the back of the study hall, and observe what goes on there. He would hear discussions, arguments, positions refuted, alternatives offered, but most of all he'd hear questions, questions, and more questions. 'How do you know?' 'What is you proof?' 'Maybe it's the opposite!'

"And that's how the learning takes place throughout — questioning not only peers, but also teachers, senior rabbis, and even the head of the seminary. No one is sacred, no one is protected from questions, questions, and more questions. Frankly, Lisa, in the scenario I suggested, I think that priest would faint. In fact, I'd expect him to blurt out, 'What is all this questioning, probing, and more questioning? Just accept the answers, have faith. The head Rabbi said this is the way it is, just accept it. Just believe!' I would expect him to walk out shaking his head and muttering something like, 'Those guys really have no faith.'

"And Lisa, the priest would be right. But it isn't that we don't have faith; it's that Torah study isn't about faith but rather about understanding, straining our mind to the ultimate level until we are able to grasp things on a deeper and more sophisticated level.

"Judaism isn't based on blind faith, it's based on understanding. While it is true that each word of the Torah is accepted as absolute truth, as it is the word of God and emanated from Him on Mount Sinai, our job is to understand every word, to delve down into its depths. The Torah was given to us to explore, to probe, to grasp as deeply as we are able. There is no faith here; there is utter knowledge, intellectual probing to the maximum depth of our understanding.

"So just for the fun of it, let's imagine there's this meeting of the rabbis, as you suggested, Lisa, where they decide to change things, to put some things in, take others out. A vote is held and all of the rabbis agree. Each one goes back to his hometown to spread the news. Each rabbi would gather his townsmen — the sages and scholars, the laymen who are adept at Torah studies, as well as the simpler laborers — and he would begin explaining the new way.

"We would expect him to say something like, 'My dear friends and colleagues, there has been a new revelation. From now on the Torah as you know it is no longer acceptable.'

"What do you think the reaction of the crowd would be? These are people trained from the cradle to analyze, to scrutinize, and to probe. Since childhood they have been accepting nothing, taking nothing for granted, always questioning and demanding proof. No fact is beyond debate; no rabbi or scholar is beyond being challenged.

"Now, along comes their rabbi with a new revelation: 'My friends, things are very different now; the old is out, and now there is a new edition of our holy Torah. The very basis of our belief system has changed. We must all accept these new descriptions of events and laws, without asking, without questioning. What is more, from now on we must accept that the old way never happened. When we teach our children, we must forget all of the old traditions, we must teach them this new way only, and we must teach them not to question it. And we will brook no dissention, because the council of rabbis to which I belong has decided that this is the best way to guarantee Jewish continuity.'

"What do you think the reaction would be? You see, Lisa, the very nature of Torah study — its insistence on analysis and striving for truth, doesn't allow for someone to come along and change what we received on Mount Sinai. The very system of transmission — and the intellectual rigor of its retransmission to the next generation — doesn't allow for falsification.

"When the Jews from Yemen came to Israel in the 1950s, they brought their Torah scrolls with them. This was a segment of our people that had been isolated from mainstream Judaism for approximately a thousand years. For all of that time, there had been no known contact between that community and the rest of the world's Jewish population. Needless to say, there was great curiosity to see the differences between the Torah scrolls in Israel currently, and the ones that had just been brought from Yemen. When they compared the newly arrived scrolls to those that existed in the Western world — ones that had come to Israel from Germany, Poland, and Russia — in all the scrolls there was only one letter in one word that was different (the pronunciation of the two words was the same, it was only a question of spelling).

"Keep in mind that Torah scrolls are handwritten. There were no photocopies or printing plates — a scribe sitting down to write a scroll would take as long as a year to complete the task. Yet there was only one letter in the entire work that was different from the ones that came from communities from which they had been separated for centuries! One letter in one word! One Torah scroll copied from another, generation after generation, over a span of more than a thousand years, and there is less deviation than even one complete word, even though there was no cross-referencing, no way of checking, and certainly none of the computer programs that are now available to verify accuracy. The transmission was so reliable that it remained perfect and intact. The reason for this is that the Torah plays a hugely important role in the lives of our people, and the exactness of every word is part of the tradition that we have from Mount Sinai.

"Think about it. We in the USA live in a country that is slightly over two hundred years old. Ask any school-age child how this nation came about, and they will recount the entire story of how we won our independence from Great Britain. How do we know that

England really taxed the colonies without offering them representation? How do we know that there was a Revolutionary War? Maybe it was just propaganda created in the Cold War era to glorify the Founding Fathers of our country and to bolster democratic ideology against the onslaught of Communism?

"The one answer to all these questions is that when something is so public, you can't suppress it, word gets out. People tell people who chronicle it and write it down. Articles are written, books are published, and the truth is known. When the identical report comes from so many different sources, there is no room for error. One person may make up a story, ten people might embellish it, but when you have thousands upon thousands of eye witnesses to an event, there is no room for doubt. That is how events become a part of history.

"Is there anyone who doubts that Alexander the Great ruled the earth and died very young, nearly thirty-three years old? That happened an awfully long time ago — maybe he only ruled over one country and died at age sixty? Maybe he never existed at all! Maybe someone made up a fable to teach the virtue of ambition! Even though it happened so long ago, something that is so public and so well-known gets written down in history, and is taught as truth to this day.

"Lisa," I said, "we as a people should be especially sensitive to this subject. We don't have to go very far back in our history to find people denying events that we know happened. Today there are books, articles, and entire websites dedicated to proving that the Holocaust never occurred. They claim that reports of a Holocaust were part of a plot by international Jewry to garner world sympathy so that the State of Israel could come into existence.

"How do we answer them? What is our response? Even if you tell me that they don't deserve an answer because they speak out of hatred and have no interest in truth — still, what is our response to those who honestly want to know? How do we *know* that the Holocaust really happened?

"To that we have a one-word response: listen. Listen as eye witness after eye witness tells his story. Listen to the accounts of entire towns being led out to dig their own graves. Listen to one woman's retelling of what it was like to watch from a hidden vantage point as huge trucks filled with Jews, many of them her closest relatives, were pumped full of lethal gas at Treblinka before the Nazis had a chance to design and build gas chambers. Listen as one man describes what it was like to stand at the door of the gas chambers of Auschwitz and be forced to pry apart the dead bodies so they could be taken to the crematoria to be incinerated. Listen to the thousands of men, women, and children with numbers tattooed on their arms, telling you of the horror they barely survived. And then ask yourself one question: Is it possible for so many people, from so many different walks of life, from so many different cultures, and from so many different nationalities to perpetrate such a fraud? Would it work? Could it ever be pulled off?

"We don't *believe* the Holocaust happened; we *know* it. We know it because of the people who were there, who survived, and now tell us what happened to them, their loved ones, and their communities. We may not have been there, but we know with absolute knowledge what happened there.

"Lisa, that's the same way that we know the Torah came from Hashem — because three million people couldn't lie and get away with it. There is no possible way that such a remarkably public event could have been fabricated and put on the record — then or at any time later in history. There is no possible way that such an occurrence could be passed down from generation to generation, talked about, studied, and discussed if it were fictional. Even more than that, there is no way to falsify a belief that has been held as precious as life itself, and as such was handed down father to son, mother to daughter, from time immemorial.

"Over millennia, Jews have willingly given up their lives for their belief in Hashem and their belief in the revelation at Sinai. Sane, rational people from every walk of life and from every type of community were willing to lay down their lives for these convictions. When facing imminent death, a parent turns to her child and says, 'My daughter, I may not know much, but this I know: there is a God in heaven, who appeared to us on Mount Sinai and gave us the Torah. I know this because my mother told me, and in turn her mother heard it from her mother — mother to daughter, mother to daughter, all the way back in an unbroken chain.' When a child hears this at such a pivotal time, she knows that it's the truth. And if it isn't simply one mother, but a nation of mothers and fathers all telling the same story to their children who they might never see again, all describing what their parents told them, who were in turn told by their parents, all the way back in time, then we know it is true.

"So, to summarize, if you ask me, do I believe that the Torah was given by Hashem to the Jewish people on Mount Sinai? The answer is no, I don't believe it, I *know* it. Much like any fact in history isn't something that we believe in but is something we know to be true. We know that the Magna Carta was the charter of English political and civil liberties granted by King John at Runnymede in June 1215. That isn't something that we accept upon faith, it's something that we *know* to be true. So too we know that an event as public as Hashem speaking to millions of people at the foot of Mount Sinai is something that can't be falsified. That event was chronicled and recorded in exacting detail, and in that form passed down in an unbroken chain, spanning millennia. It's not something that we believe in, it is something we know.

"That was a rather long answer to a short question, but an important subject. Why don't we stop here, Lisa?" I asked. "I don't know what your schedule looks like, but you are more than welcome to join us next week as well."

"I'd love to," she replied. "But be forewarned: I still have lots of questions!"

Chapter Nineteen

PEOPLE BELIEVE WHAT
THEY WANT TO BELIEVE

A s Lisa and David settled in for our talk, I expected a barrage of questions from Lisa, but instead David said, "I had an interesting encounter this week, Rabbi, and I thought that you would be the right person to discuss it with. One evening Lisa and I were having dinner with a friend whom I haven't seen in quite some time, and the conversation turned to my increased interest in religion. I told him that I was studying with a rabbi, and we were getting into some of the fundamentals of man's purpose in this world, when he asked, 'Do you actually believe in God?'

"I said, 'Sure I do.'

"He then said that he'd spent a lot of time thinking about this, and he just didn't see how people could believe in God. How can you possibly believe in something that you can't see, something so remote, something that is so far removed from what we experience day to day?'

"The conversation got heated when he said to me, 'If you really believe in God, prove to me that He exists.' And, Rabbi, to be honest, as much as I tried, I didn't succeed. It seemed that no matter what I said, he didn't accept my position. I have to admit that I left that dinner feeling frustrated."

I sat back in my chair for a moment and then said, "A few years back, I was teaching one of my weekly Bible study classes in the synagogue, when a bright young man, who was then in dental school, made a comment that I can't forget. He said, 'All of the miracles that we have been studying are very impressive — the ancient Egyptians being smitten with the plagues, then the splitting of the sea, and all the miracles that happened in the desert. It's all great, Rabbi, but that happened so long ago. What I need is for God to show me just one miracle. Today. Right now. Then I would believe in Him.'

"I thought about his remark for some time, until I realized that he had stumbled upon one of the very basic tenets of our belief system.

"I asked my young friend if he thought that miracles make a person believe in God. He answered, 'Of course! Anyone would believe if they had seen the type of miracles described in the Bible.'

"I said to him, 'I have one simple question. If what you say is true, that witnessing miracles forces one to believe in God, why didn't the ancient Egyptians abandon their idol worship and become believers?'

"'What do you mean?' he replied. 'They weren't impressed by miracles because they were wicked; they were the ones who wanted to kill the Jews.'

"'I understand,' I said to him, 'but they experienced the very same miracles that the Jewish nation did. They lived through the entire Ten Plagues, which took place over one full year. They saw the same manifestation of God's might as the Jews did, yet the vast majority of them never came to any recognition of God's dominion. Quite the opposite — until their bitter, watery end most of them denied

God. According to your thesis that miracles make a person believe in God, how could that be? How could a nation live through such obvious and clear miracles and not believe?'

"To put this question into more precise focus, let's imagine what it was like to be an Egyptian at that time. Let's picture Anat, a simple, reasonably honest, hard-working land owner standing in the hot sun wondering how he is going to get his cows to market. Along comes his friend Djeti.

"'Say, Anat, did you hear what's going on?' Djeti asks.

"'No, what?'

"'Well, this tall, majestic Hebrew named Moses marched into the palace with his brother, Aaron, and started threatening King Pharaoh.'

"'Hey, he can't be too bright,' Anat responds. 'Remember what happened to the last guy who tried that? Pharaoh's wife is now using his dried bones as clothespins.'

"'Right! Anyway, this Moses fellow says that God sent him to tell Pharaoh to let the Sons of Jacob go.'

"'Which god sent him?'

"'Not any that we recognize. Moses is talking about this super God, Whom he says created the heavens and earth, and still runs everything.'

"'What do you expect, Djeti? Everyone thinks that their god is the best.'

"'No, you don't understand. This Moses did all these freaky things. First, he flung his staff down to the ground and it turned into a snake. Then he put his hand in his shirt, and it came out white with leprosy. After that, he spilled water on the ground and it turned into blood. And here's the kicker — he threatened that if Pharaoh doesn't let the Jews go, this God of his is going to turn all of the water in all of Egypt into...blood!'

"'Come now, Djeti, do you really believe even one word of what you're telling me?'

"'Well, I may or may not believe it. But I'll tell you this much, Pharaoh sure took him seriously.'

"Now, Anat worshipped his fair share of idols, not really sure that he believed in any of them, but why take chances, right? So he makes sure to stash away a couple of extra barrels of water, just in case.

"Then, on the day that Moses predicted, and at the exact time as well, lo and behold, all the water in all of Egypt turns into blood. Not just the water in the Nile, but also the water in the kitchens, the bathtubs, the barrels, the fields — all the water anywhere to be found — turns into blood. If an Egyptian had water stored in the basement, it turned to blood; if he stored some in a jug in his attic, it turned to blood. If he bit into a fruit, instead of juice he got a spurt of blood.

"Let's keep in mind that blood isn't just red-colored water, it's thick and it has a distinct, metallic odor. Wherever there had been water, it was now blood — except for water owned by Jews. If a Jewish person was drinking water, it remained water.

"Now, let us imagine that our friend Anat has a few Jewish slaves, one of whom is working in his field that day. While watching what's going on all around him, Anat says to himself, 'I may not be the sharpest triangle in the pyramid, but even I can figure out that something is going on here.' He calls over his Jewish slave, who is happily drinking a glass of cool, refreshing water.

"'Hey, Isaac, come here!'

"'Yes, Master.'

"'What's that you're drinking?'

"'Water, sir.'

"'Yeah, that's what I thought. Now wipe that smirk off your face, and give me some of it.'

"So the Jewish slave hands over the cup of water, and as the cup passes from his hand to the hand of his Egyptian master, the water turns into blood.

"'Hey, take that back!' Anat screams.

"As Isaac takes back the cup, it turns from blood to water.

"Anat shouts, 'Now give me back the water!'

"Again, no sooner does the cup leave Isaac's hand then it turns to blood. And this goes on, back and forth: water...blood, water... blood, water...blood.

"Finally, Anat thinks for a moment and says, 'Now, listen here! You and I are going to drink at the same time! Go to the kitchen and bring out two glass straws, and we'll both sip water from your glass together. And remember — no tricks, or I will whip you bloody, understand?!'

"They both stand together, ready to sip from the cup.

"'Ready. One, two, three... Ughhhhhh!' Anat shrieks, spitting out blood, while his slave, Isaac, swallows clear, fresh water.

"Now, that's a very impressive feat. It isn't every day that all of the water in all of Egypt turns into blood. Every person living in Egypt saw clearly and directly that Hashem is the One Who controls nature. How else could liquid change from one state to another, depending upon who was holding it? The message that Hashem was delivering as clear as day was that blood is red and thick because He so decrees it should be. The minute Hashem decrees that it should be otherwise, it changes to clear, pure drinking water. There is no such thing as the laws of nature existing independently of Hashem. Rather, those are the rules and guidelines that He uses to run His world, but the moment He sees fit to change them, it is as if those 'laws' never existed.

"The Egyptians weren't being exposed to some theoretical spiritual concept. This miracle, if you will, was something that every Egyptian man, woman, and child clearly saw. During this first of the Ten Plagues, they lived through an undeniable demonstration of Hashem's control over every facet of nature. And they experienced Hashem's presence in their everyday life — not a million miles away, up in heaven, but as the saying goes, 'up close and personal.' And yet, they did not abandon their idols and pledge allegiance to the One God, the Creator.

"What is even more astounding is that Hashem could have taken the Jewish nation out of Egypt in any manner He chose. The reason He chose to do it this way was to make it clear for all to see that He is a force to be reckoned with, so that anyone witnessing these events would come to the inescapable conclusion that there is one, and only one, Almighty God in the world Who controls and runs it. That was to be the one time in history when Hashem would openly demonstrate His dominion over nature, so that all future generations should be able to point back to that moment as a basis of their belief in Him.

"Yet the amazing fact was that the Egyptians did not come to that belief! They lived through all the miracles of the Ten Plagues, saw the Hand of God right before their eyes, and still they didn't abandon their idols and begin worshipping the Almighty God. Until the bitter end, almost all of the Egyptians denied His existence and power.

"We have to ask ourselves how that could be. How could intelligent, reasonable people see such clear manifestations of Hashem's might, and not believe in Him?

"If we spend time reviewing some of the events that transpired in that era, I think we will find this question even more perplexing.

"The Bible very clearly states that before each plague, Moses came to Pharaoh's palace and warned him exactly what was going to happen. Each time Moses gave a warning, not only did the plague happen, but it happened exactly *as* he said it would, *when* he said it would.

"At that time, Egypt was the most powerful nation in the world; it was also by far the wealthiest. As an agricultural society, their wealth was only as great as the riches produced by their fields and flocks. During the next ten months, as each plague caused the unprecedented destruction of both, they suffered ruinous financial disaster. Little by little, their resources and all the reserves they had built up through the years were wiped out. Their fields were empty of produce, and all of their livestock died. Each plague was specifically designed to demonstrate that every facet of nature is directly controlled by Hashem, and each plague highlighted another dimension of that control.

"Before the last plague, Moses had a captive audience. The Egyptians had now lived through ten months of warnings and devastating plagues, and they were finally convinced that every time Moses promised that something would happen, it did — exactly as he had predicted, down to the minutest detail. At that point, there were enough Egyptians who, by witnessing Hashem's many miracles, actually did believe in Him. A group of firstborn Egyptians came to Pharaoh's palace and presented the king with an ultimatum: either let the Jews go, or we will dethrone you. Not only didn't Pharaoh heed their ultimatum, he slaughtered the entire group, which effectively ended the uprising.

"Then, at the appointed time, in the appointed manner, every firstborn in Egypt died.

"Whether the oldest-born child was five or fifty-five, he died. Whether there was one son or ten, only the oldest died. And in a house where there were six boys ranging in age from sixteen to twenty-six — and the next-to-oldest was taller, stronger, and looked five years older than his oldest brother — only the actual firstborn died.

"But it wasn't only the firstborn who died; the Bible clearly states that there wasn't an Egyptian house that didn't suffer a death. The Talmud elucidates by stating that if there was a firstborn male child in the home, he died; if not, then the oldest male in the house died. So if a particular home had only girls, the father died.

"Who was keeping track of which son was oldest? Who had recorded which one of twin boys emerged first? It was clear to everyone living in Egypt that Hashem watches over every living creature and records all, that nothing escapes His notice.

"What is even more compelling is that in many houses there was more than one death. The commentaries explain that Egyptian women were not exactly paragons of virtue. So you might have a house in which, over the years, a woman — we'll call her Dendera — bore children from a number of men. Each child that was the firstborn of his father died, which means that some mothers witnessed the deaths of several of her sons.

"Let's imagine for a moment Dendera's feelings as she buries four of her sons on one day! What does she say to herself? 'How could anyone have known who was the father of which child? How could anyone have known they were all firstborn children to different fathers? It's been decades! For twenty-five years I've been keeping this secret. Each son died! What does this mean? What is happening? How could this possibly be? Woe to a mother who suffers such tragedy!'

"What Dendera saw with absolute clarity was that Hashem knew everything. He is ever-present and watches every event that transpires on the face of this planet. Dendera saw clearly that everything is recorded, weighed, and measured. Very few accounts are settled immediately, but in the end Hashem metes out absolute justice. Often, this doesn't happen until years later, but in the end, the Someone Who watches settles all accounts.

"The amazing part of all of this is that Dendera didn't learn this through some theoretical lecture about morality and God. She didn't attend a course in esoteric philosophy that has little bearing on her life. She saw it and felt it with exacting, painful clarity. It happened to her and it was real.

"Can we imagine the extent to which Dendera now understood the control and sovereignty that Hashem maintains over the world?

But don't be surprised that even this level of revelation didn't effect the slightest change in her beliefs. Listen as we walk with Dendera to the cemetery as she prepares to bury her four grown sons. Hush, she's speaking with some of the other women mourners: 'You know, girls, this just strengthens what I have always said to you, we must be so careful about our health! Early death comes swiftly to those who don't watch their cholesterol, get yearly checkups, and exercise regularly. Why, just look what happened to my four sons. Oh, the tragedy of it all! Please, girls, promise me — no more red meat!'

"There are not enough words to describe our amazement over the rank stupidity of such a statement! Is it possible to even imagine that an intelligent human being — someone who looks, speaks, and thinks like you or me — could ever utter such drivel?

"But, in reality, that is the equivalent of what the Egyptians did. Even after the final and worst plague, even after all the otherworldly miracles they witnessed, did they now believe? Did they now admit the futility of their idol worship? Did they say, 'We were wrong and we now repent'? No! Not only didn't they admit the error of their ways, but they actually chased after the Jewish nation and followed them into the sea, bent on annihilating them! Is there a way to make some sense out of such stupid behavior? What does it say about humankind when, after experiencing the Ten Plagues, a sophisticated nation went to their deaths without even awakening to the realization that maybe, just maybe, there is a living God in this world Whose forgiveness they should seek?

"I am sure that by now both of you understand that these people were exercising their Free Will to either believe in or deny God. Both of you by now also realize that we humans have a fantastic ability to believe what we want to believe, irrespective of logic or truth. And by now you'll both surely admit that if people don't want to believe, you can show them irrefutable evidence, you can perform the most blatant miracles, and they still won't change their minds.

"We humans have this uncanny ability not to be moved by truth and logic, but by emotions and desires. As part of the Master Plan for creation, Hashem gave us this ability to believe what we want to believe, no matter the number of miracles we witness.

"As a religious person, this is something that I experience on a daily basis. I look at a world that is so vast, so diverse, and yet so harmonious in all of its complexity. From the cosmic dimension of hundreds upon hundreds of billions of stars all moving in controlled orbits, down to the subatomic contents of each cell, all components meshing in such mind-numbing symmetry and accord, all screaming out the undeniable fact that there is a Creator and Master of this world. Yet we find rational, intelligent people saying things like, 'It just happened,' 'By luck,' 'By chance,' and, 'If only I saw a miracle, I'd believe.'

"I remember when my wife was expecting our fourth child, it became a favorite project between us to calculate the development of the unborn fetus. Looking at pictures of embryos at different stages of development, we would imagine what stage our unborn family member had reached. It was a moving experience to watch the progress of a human baby forming; we saw such wisdom in it all. From the beginning of the nubs that were to become the limbs, to the forming of the spinal cortex, the entire development of this vastly complex organism was all so controlled, so orchestrated — the most sophisticated explosion of life, all happening far away from the human eye. To my wife and me, it was a very moving religious experience.

"Our baby was born on Yom Kippur. There I was, a young rabbi dressed in my holiday finest, frantically rushing my wife to the hospital. As I stood there in the delivery room, I felt a rush of emotion as I witnessed this miracle called birth — the most magnificent, stupendous occurrence, the bringing forth of life, happening on our most holy day. I felt as high as a kite. Thank God, everything went well, the baby was a healthy, fully formed, beautiful girl. I was so appreciative of this gift of life that I wanted to sing aloud several Psalms of thanksgiving.

"At that moment, when my mind was overflowing with gratitude to Hashem for what He had blessed us with, I said to the nurse, 'Wow, what a miracle!' to which she answered, 'Yes, isn't it wonderful how nature has evolved?'

"Now, this wasn't the time for a philosophical debate, so I didn't comment. But it brought home my point more clearly than anything I experienced before or after. Here was a woman who, on a daily basis, was involved in one of the most miraculous events of creation — she participated in and helped to bring forth new life. Is there anyone who can deny the holiness of such an event?

"Is there anyone who isn't awed by the magnificence of a fully formed human baby growing from specks of nothingness so small that they were once invisible to the naked eye? All of the wisdom of the human body encoded in the subatomic DNA, a microcomputer housed in each cell, controlling the formation of millions upon millions of cells, some becoming part of the bone structure, others forming organs, and yet others developing into the gray matter that comprises the human brain. Do we have adequate words to describe the wonder of it all? And not only didn't she see anything special about it, to her it was just another cog in the evolutionary process.

"Yes, we repeatedly see that while there is great debate among scientists, there remains a core of individuals who, despite a world full of evidence to the contrary, affirm that there is no Creator, that the world evolved by chance, by random luck, nothing but a roll of the cosmic dice.

"I don't want to get into an entire discussion about evolution right now, maybe at some future time we can. But one point I do want to make is that if the greatest supernatural miracles ever shown to man couldn't convince Egyptian society that there is a God Who created the world and retains mastery of it, it shouldn't surprise us to find intelligent, well-read people in our midst who can look at the miracles of creation and birth and deny Hashem. And the reason this is so has to do with the very nature of the human psyche.

"One of the most memorable characters of the old TV show called *Star Trek* was Mr. Spock. He was the fellow with pointy ears, the Vulcan. While everyone else on the spacecraft *Enterprise* was subject to human emotions, he came from a different planet and was only capable of thinking logically. In fact, he couldn't understand emotions — if it wasn't logical, you didn't do it. We tend to think of ourselves as human Mr. Spocks. We assume that our approach to life situations is totally logical, totally thought out. We work with this unspoken assumption that our emotions, the ways in which we feel, don't alter the way we view major issues. Unfortunately, we couldn't be more mistaken.

"As much as we hate to admit it, even to ourselves, *most* of our decisions and choices are made based solely on emotion. To show you what I mean, try and remember the latest Marlboro cigarette billboards you've seen. All that appears is an oversized picture of the Marlboro Man — skin as thick as leather, face so tight that it would crack if he smiled. And the focus of it all: the white cancer stick dangling from his lips. Whether you noticed or not, there is not even a mention of the cigarette brand!

"Did you ever wonder why the ad guys designed it that way? Why don't they just present a whole bunch of logical statements, like: 'Our cigarettes are the best' or, 'For the finest flavor and taste, eight out of ten smokers prefer our brand of cigarettes to any other'? Wouldn't that be the logical way to sell cigarettes?

"Truthfully, that would be the *logical* way to market that product. But advertisers know full well that logic doesn't sell anything — because consumers don't buy based on logic, they buy based on *emotions*. The implication in the Marlboro advertisement is clear: If you want to be cool, if you want to be macho like the Marlboro Man, you need to smoke Marlboro. They really aren't selling their brand of cigarettes, they are selling something much more in demand, something much more basic to human wants and desires. They are selling *prestige*. Be cool, be macho, smoke Marlboro.

"Now, you may ask if this really works. Is anyone really gullible enough to fall for that? After all, I go to work every day in a suit, not a cowboy outfit. I drive a car, I don't ride a powerful horse. I don't wear boots and stirrups, but the latest in sports shoes. So is anyone going to say, 'Boy, I want to be just like the Marlboro Man, sitting up there so strong and handsome, with skin hard as leather, so I better run down to the store and get myself a pack right now.' Who in their right mind is going to say that to themselves, and then buy a pack of cancer sticks?

"The answer is: no one in their right mind. But it doesn't matter, because Madison Avenue knows that no one makes decisions 'in their right mind.' Most of our decisions as consumers are made in our deeply recessed subconscious, the part of us that wants things, the part of us that craves things. When I decide to buy this model car or that one, rarely does it have to do with performance and function; it has to do with perceptions and feelings. Is this *my kind* of car? What does that model *mean* to me? How will I *feel* when I drive around in it? How does driving this kind of car *position me* among my friends and neighbors? Most of my purchases touch upon a part of me that is deeply hidden — my emotional makeup — and that part of me isn't limited to the rules of logic and sensibility.

"Granted, I may rationalize my decision, I may come up with very solid arguments to support my choice. But if we are brutally honest with ourselves, we admit that most of our decision to buy a particular product is made based on how we feel about the item. The rational arguments are an afterthought to defend my choice to my logical thinking side.

"Our emotions affect us more than we care to admit. They affect our decisions of what we buy, they influence our opinion as to who we vote for, and the way that we feel about things can even affect what we believe in.

"To illustrate this point, Rabbi Elchonon Wasserman, one of Judaism's great leaders during the first half of the twentieth century, asks a powerful philosophical question: The Bible gives us a specific commandment to believe in God; Rabbi Elchonon asks how Hashem can command us to believe something. If I already believe in God, then I don't need a commandment to do so. And if I don't believe in Him, how will a commandment help? The Bible can command me to do an action — to give charity, or to help a widow. I might not wish to, I might not be in the mood, but if there is a direct command from Hashem, hopefully I will do it anyway. But with the commandment to believe, we are dealing with something that is totally elusive, something that is in my heart. If my heart doesn't believe, what shall I tell it? 'Heart, you must believe. Hashem commanded you to believe, so just do it!' Obviously, this won't work. So what's the point of this commandment?

"His answer is as profound as it is simple. He says that the Torah isn't commanding a person to believe in God, per se. Rather, the commandment is: Be honest. Be open. Look at the world, see its beauty, its diversity, its complexity, and ask yourself: 'Honestly, what do you think? Do you think that this complex world actually just happened? Do you think it made itself?'

"Often, our agendas get in the way of our thinking. If I accept God's existence, it means that I have been wrong up until now, and that runs against my grain. If I accept God, then there are going to be things I may have to do, or things that I will not be able to do. Therefore, it's just so much easier, so much more convenient, if I continue proclaiming that there is no God.

"You see," I concluded, "I don't think we are accustomed to thinking honestly. We have our preconceived notions, our own worldview, and everything that we come across gets filtered through those preset assumptions. If we find input that supports our position, we latch on to it. If we find conclusions we are uncomfortable with, no matter how logically compelling they may be, we find reasons to reject them. Our wants and desires color everything we see and distort our vision. What the Bible tells us is to set aside all of our entrenched notions and approach the question — does God exist? — from an intellectual vantage point. Bottom line: what do you honestly think?

"If you have a discussion with someone and he says, 'Prove that God exists,' his real intention will determine whether you will succeed. If what he means is, 'I am open; I have questions and honestly want to hear the answers,' then it's a relatively simple matter to show such a person the Hand of God in our infinitely complex and well-integrated world. Could such a fantastic universe have simply come into being on its own? Doesn't the 'house' scream out the existence of its 'architect'?

"But if what he is really saying is, 'I refuse to believe in God. I find it too difficult to change my perspective and my day-to-day life and I don't want to hear what you are saying,' then there is no way that you can convince him. The most logically compelling arguments and the most irrefutable facts won't move him because what he is really saying is, 'My mind is made up; I already know the correct answer.' Just like the Egyptians.

"If, in fact, he was Mr. Spock, and his actions, thoughts, and decisions were based on logic, then it would be an easy enough task to convince him. But the reality is that we humans just don't function that way. So, David, short of handcuffing your old friend's mind to a position that he refuses to hear, there is no way to prove to him that God exists, or for that matter to convince him of any other position that he doesn't want to hear.

"And that is why the Ancient Egyptians didn't believe in God despite having seen ten unbelievable miracles that were absolutely irrefutable, despite having seen the Hand of God, and despite witnessing unprecedented miracles that were so undeniable that they are the underpinning of our faith. They saw and didn't believe, because Hashem created us with this fantastic ability to believe only what we want to believe. And that is why even if we were to witness miracles today, if we are predisposed against believing in Hashem, we wouldn't necessarily change our position.

"This all stems from this one phenomenon — that people don't believe what is logical and true. We aren't Mr. Spock. At the end of the day, people only believe what they want to believe."

"Rabbi," Lisa said, "what you are proposing is that the average person can lie to himself and live in a world of delusion, simply inventing things to suit his interests and somehow fooling himself into believing them."

"Exactly."

"Sorry, Rabbi, I don't view things that way. Maybe my professional training has had too strong an influence on me, but that's my reality. I work under the assumption that if something is true, any human would have to admit to it — if the facts were presented to them in a logical, well-documented fashion. How can a person who is wise, clear-headed, and insightful believe things that he knows aren't true just because he wants to?"

Chapter Twenty

I NEVER DO ANYTHING WRONG

"OK," I said. "You're saying that the majority of people are rational and that if something is true they will recognize it, while I suggested that there's a much more complex mechanism involved, and that the type of thinking I described is far more common than we like to admit. Let's discuss. Here's an interesting example: In the 1930s, one of the most notorious gangsters who ever shot up the streets of New York City was called Two-Gun Crowley. He was also known as 'Crowley the Cop Killer.' The police commissioner at the time described him as one of the most ruthless, hardened killers who ever walked the streets of New York, a teenager who killed just for the fun of it!

"Two-Gun fired his last bullet in a shoot-out with police in an apartment on Manhattan's West Ninety-First Street. Surrounded by 150 policemen who used everything from tear gas to machine guns mounted on surrounding rooftops, he still managed to hold them at bay for over an hour. More than ten thousand onlookers watched from the streets and open tenement building windows as sounds of machine-gun fire turned the area into what sounded like a battlefield. Finally, after being shot in the chest, he wrote his last message, a note drenched in his blood, which read: 'To whom it may concern: Under my coat lies a lonely heart, but a good heart, a heart that would do no man harm.'

"And he signed it!

"Only hours before he had been sitting in a car with his girl-friend. When one of two passing police officers asked him for his license and registration, Two-Gun reached into his coat, pulled out a revolver, and shot the cop dead. He then jumped out of the car, grabbed the officer's service revolver, shot the dead policeman once more for good measure, shot the officer's partner, and drove off. He could just as easily have sped off without shooting either of the policemen, but he didn't — 'a good heart, a heart that would do no man harm.'

"Our story doesn't end here. Two-Gun Crowley managed to survive the shoot-out in Manhattan. The police broke in, arrested him, he stood trial, and was sentenced to death. On his way to the electric chair, he was overheard saying, 'This is what I get for defending myself.'

"What makes this story significant for our discussion is that I don't think that Two-Gun Crowley was insane, or that his self-perception was a sign of dementia. In fact, his behavior seems to be quite common among criminals. In one of Dale Carnegie's books, he writes that he had an ongoing correspondence with the warden of Sing Sing prison, who explained to him that not one of his inmates admitted that he was guilty. Every one of them had some reason why he had to be quick on the trigger, or why he had to live a life of crime. I think this holds true in every segment of the population. No one thinks of themselves as evil or bad, or even that they do things that are wrong.

"It seems that this type of thought process is common among thieves. The viewpoint of most criminals is: 'Everyone would steal. The only reason other people don't steal is because they aren't as bright as I am — they just aren't as bold. But believe me, if they were as sharp as me, they would be out there stealing all day long.'

"We may call this rationalizing, or we might call it a defense mechanism, but there is a fundamental reason why we human beings do this, and it has to do with the very definition of Free Will.

"Let me explain:

"Lisa," I said, "do you have Free Will to put your hand in a fire?"

"Do I have Free Will?"

"Yes," I said. "Let's say I offer you a hundred dollars to put your hand in a fire, do you have Free Will to do it?"

"Well, I guess I do," Lisa answered. "But I sure don't think that I would!"

"Your answer is very accurate; you have Free Will, but you wouldn't do it because it's a stupid, self-destructive thing for you to do. When we talk about Free Will, we don't mean the *theoretical ability* to do something. We mean there has to be a real challenge, a real fight. Both sides have to be appealing, both choices have to have merit, and the human must be able to go either way.

"The problem is that if man were created with these two parts only, there would be no Free Will because the spiritual soul of man is so pure, it simply won't allow him to do something wrong. It would never allow him to do something selfish or cruel or mean. It would rebel and scream, 'How could you do that? That's nasty. You're hurting another human being! What right do you have to put your self-interests before another person's?' Granted, he would have the *physical ability* to do things that were wrong, but he wouldn't do them, much as you wouldn't put your hand in a fire.

"And therein lies one of the greatest dilemmas in creation: How do you take this pinnacle of greatness, man, who has a spiritual soul that is considered holier than an angel, and counterbalance that loftiness? If the goal is to have a level playing field, where man can truly exercise his Free Will, how do you create a balance against that majestic spiritual soul?

"To solve this thorny dilemma, Hashem, in His infinite wisdom, gave man just such a balancing agent, what we call 'imagination.' When Hashem created man, not only did He implant in him a spiritual and an animal Soul, He also introduced this third component of imagination to interplay between the two. This quality of imagination serves as an equalizer between our logical thought processes and our emotions.

"Thanks to this third component, when man approaches an issue, he isn't only limited to pure thought. Now, the very way he looks at things is subjective. If I want something, if I desire it, my emotions can affect my entire way of understanding that issue. No longer is it something that I know is wrong but want to do anyway. I now have this ability to create — almost by instinct — entire rationales that change my view. My emotions color my opinions and thought processes and affect the very way that I view life. And now my sense of morality is no longer set in concrete, but can change at will because I no longer think only with my logical side; I also have this component of creative imagination that mixes into my very thought process. Now man can, in fact, do exactly as he wants. If he wishes to choose selfish interests, his spiritual soul can't stop him because in his convoluted mind, whatever he does is right.

"So when that Voice Inside screams out, 'Do something meaningful with your life!' now there is an answer: 'I am doing something. I am doing something noble and proper and right. And it is so, because I will it to be! Because in my mind's eye I see that it is.'

"And now, finally, I truly have Free Will. Free from the shackles of having to do what is right because that higher side of me demands it from me; free to chart my course in life exactly as I see fit. If my agenda is self-serving aggrandizement, in a flash I can create an entire thought process that not only justifies this, but reframes it so that to me it appears to be something grand. I am no longer restricted to doing only what my spiritual soul tells me is right, because now I have the ability to change my understanding of what is right and what is wrong. Now I am no longer restricted by the rules of logic, as guided by absolute truth; instead, I am free to shape that logic. I can rationalize and create entire philosophies that, at least on a certain level, I believe. And since I make the rules of what is right and wrong, no one, not even my Voice Inside, can lecture me. Now I am truly free to choose my course in life because not only do I have Free Will in how I act, I now have Free Will in what I believe. **Finally, I can believe what I want to believe.**

"This is something that happens all the time. We may not focus on it, but we have this inborn capacity to believe things that we know aren't true. Think of a movie. The hero is walking down a deserted alleyway. The tempo of the music quickens. The alleyway gets darker, and shadows play against the rough, brick wall. You sense the danger, you feel the impending doom. Then it happens. Three guys jump out. Our hero gets hit. He falls to the ground. One guy hits him. Another jumps on his back. He rolls. He punches. The first thug crumples up in pain. Punch. Kick. Punch. Kick. The thirds thug jumps into the fight. Your pulse quickens; you feel your heart pounding. 'Come on, hit him! Duck! Now, kick him!' you scream.

"If we were to stop now and take your pulse, it would be racing, and your hands would be cold and sweaty. Now ask yourself one very simple question: what's going on here? This is a movie. Those are paid actors up there on the screen. You know that. You know they aren't really hitting each other, it's made up, it's pretend. So why are you sweating? And even more, let's say it was real. Let's say there was a real honest-to-goodness fight going on, and the hero of our story was being beaten up. Still, why are you sweating? Why is your heart pounding? That's him up there getting beat up — not you.

"But it *is* you. As any casting director knows, the secret to good acting is how much the audience identifies with the actor. Meaning, how much they see *themselves* in that role. So that's not our hero who's walking down that alleyway — it is you. And it isn't our hero who is getting jumped — it is you. When you watch good acting, you find yourself intimately involved, as if it were happening to you. Have you ever cried during a movie? You didn't feel emotional because something good happened to that actor; rather, it was because in your mind it happened to you. You were there; you were living that story. It was you who just discovered the long-lost brother, it was you who was languishing in prison, and it was you who made that comeback from cancer and went on to compete in the Olympics.

"This ability to fantasize, to take something that is pure fiction and see it as if it were real, is something that Hashem implanted in us for a specific purpose: it allows us to see things as we wish them to be. With this capacity of imagination, we can believe things — things that may not be true, things that we know aren't true. But we are able to accept them as so. We have this ability to see what we want to see as if it is real, and because of this we can believe what we want to believe.

"And this phenomenon plays out in our life when we find ourselves face-to-face with something we want to do, but know is wrong. That is when our imagination, this God-given creative process, kicks in. This process of inventing entire philosophies and then believing in them begins. Imagine a young man, a high school student, who goes through something like this when he sees another fellow's money. He wants the money, and yet knows that he can't take it. So now what? Take it? *That's stealing, that's wrong. I can't do that.* Not take it? *But I want it.* And so the battle begins: two voices, each one presenting its side.

"'Come on, why don't you take that money? You can really use it, right?'

"'What, are you crazy? That's stealing! I can't do that.'

"'Come on, don't be such a Holy Roller, everybody has some faults, so this is yours. What's so bad about one little fault? We're all human, you know. Come on, now, take it.'

"'I will not! That's not the kind of person I am. I don't do those kinds of things.'

"'Look, some guys have jobs, some guys get money from their parents. Everyone has money, except you. Don't you deserve to have things as well? Who takes care of you? No one, that's who! You're all alone in this world, and if you don't take care of yourself, no one will. You don't have it easy, you know. Come on, now, take it, take the money, just do it.'

"'You're crazy, I can't take it, it belongs to Sam. Sam is my friend, I can't steal from Sam.'

"'What did Sam ever do for you? Besides, is he better than you? Did he do anything to deserve more than you? Why should he have things that you don't have? I happen to think that it's plain unfair for Sam to have more than you. Not only that, I think it's wrong. It's wrong for Sam to have more than you! The really proper thing would be for Sam to share with you. Since he hasn't offered, the only right thing is to help Sam do what he should have done on his own. So I want you to go right now and help Sam do the right thing. Go take it, it's a mitzvah!'

"Lisa," I said, "if this wasn't what actually goes on in our minds, we might have found it quite humorous. But it's not funny, because it is us. We do things just like this — all the time. We may not focus on this process, we may not even be aware of it, but it constantly functions like this. Humans come up with the most fanciful, creative rationales not only to justify what they do but to make it appear to be the right thing to do.

"The Talmud tells us, 'If a person sins once, he perceives his action as a sin. If he repeats that sin, in his mind it now changes from a sin to something permitted.' Rabbi Yisrael Salanter adds, 'What happens if he repeats that sin a third time? Then in his mind the action becomes a mitzvah, a positive commandment, something *he must do.*'

"As I get on in life, I see this over and over again. No one does anything wrong! There is always a reason, a rationale, for what I have done. 'This situation is different. The normal rules don't apply to me. What more could be expected from me? Anyone who was in my place would have done the same.' We humans have this uncanny ability to create entire worldviews, sometimes very whimsical ones, to justify what we have done. Rare is the man who can look you in the eye and say, 'I have done wrong.' Most often what we hear are stories, stories that start with excuses and end with justifications, but always consistent with one theme — 'I wasn't wrong. I was justified and correct in what I did.' And even if we hear that rare 'I was wrong,' very soon thereafter comes that ever-present caveat, 'But....'

"This situation would be interesting enough if we only did it to others, but we do it all the time to ourselves. We create these illusions, entire fantasies, with which we justify our behavior to ourselves. Why can't I just say the words, 'This is wrong! I know I shouldn't do it, but I want to do it anyway'? Those words seem almost impossible to utter. It seems as if my teeth would chatter, my skull would shake, and my entire existence would be in jeopardy if I had to admit to any guilt.

"Why? Why is it so hard? Why can't I just say, 'This is wrong! It isn't proper, I know I shouldn't do it, but I want to do it, and I am going to do it anyway'? Psychologists will use words like 'defense mechanism' and 'self-protection,' but this isn't defending me against someone else, this is what is going on inside my mind, and no one else is listening. This is a conversation between me and me, so what's the problem?

"The answer is that I have to rationalize my behavior to myself because a part of me, my spiritual soul, wouldn't stand for me doing anything wrong — it wouldn't allow it. It's that simple. I cannot and will not do something that is wrong. So there's only one choice if, in fact, I want to do it — I must make it seem right. I must invent a theory or a way of viewing things that turns something that is wrong, clearly wrong, into something OK.

"'Listen, other people do it,' 'It can't be that bad,' or 'Plenty of people do far worse things.' And if the activity is something that I do regularly, then it isn't enough for it to be OK, it has to become a good thing to do. I will create an entire thought process to explain to myself why this is not something wrong, this is really a positive act, even a service to mankind. A little mental sleight of hand, and now everything is permitted, everything is OK.

"Ridiculous? Yes. Ludicrous? Most certainly. But that is us. That's the human condition, and it's time we dealt with it. We never do anything wrong. Period. No matter what.

"Don't misunderstand me. We can make mistakes. Anyone can do that. We can even make mistakes in judgment. All that is excusable. I am speaking about things that are intrinsically wrong, things that if I did them, I would be guilty of being inconsiderate or rude or of putting my interests before someone else's. It's those types of things that you will never, ever find me doing. No matter how glaring, no matter how obvious it is to everyone else, in my mind whatever that activity was, it was 'justified and deserved.'

"The most heinous villains who ever existed all had a self-redeeming philosophy. They had a viewpoint, a way of looking at things, that not only justified what they did but made it appear to have been a good deed. Hitler didn't say, 'It is wrong to kill innocent men, women, and children, but I hate them so let's do it anyway.'

He wrote a seven-hundred-twenty-page treatise, *Mein Kampf*, in which he outlined the world's problems, particularly the problems of Germany, and how the Jews are the cause of it all. His rhetoric proves that it is a *good deed* to kill a Jew. 'Much like when one kills a mosquito, one doesn't feel remorse; it serves very little purpose in this world, it is a nuisance. So too when one kills a Jew he should have the same attitude. He should understand that he is helping rid Germany and the world of a plague, the poisoner of all people, International Jewry.'

"Do you remember the defense that almost every Nazi hid behind at the Nuremberg Trials? 'I was only following orders.' In a way, I think there is some truth to that. I don't for a minute question the horrific nature of the Nazi beasts, and I don't have an ounce of forgiveness in me for what they perpetrated against our people. And they are each individually responsible for what they did. But still, I believe that many of them truly felt that they were doing just that: 'only following orders.'

"I doubt there were many Nazis who were emotionally strong enough to justify to themselves the murder of innocent women and children. They were human, and even in them there existed a Voice Inside that screamed out: 'Hans, how can you do this? These are people, human beings just like you. They have done nothing wrong. How can you do this?'

"And there has to be some answer to that voice. A human being can't ignore that voice; he has to respond. So the truly wicked, powerfully evil members of the Nazi party shouted lines to themselves that had been drummed into their ears for years, and they believed them: 'The Jews are vermin, all that is bad in Germany is because of the Jews. It is either the Jews or the Fatherland, and I choose Germany. As one kills vermin, we kill Jews.'

"But it takes a very, very committed person to be able to believe those words of justification. What about the simple guard in

Auschwitz? What about the young fellow who just went along with the crowd? He didn't really believe that stuff; in his heart he knew it was all garbage. So what does he answer to that Voice Inside that screams out, 'What are you doing, Hans? What's going on here?! This is genocide and you are a part of it! Stop! Stop right now. Better to jump into that pit of fire yourself than to throw in one more innocent child.'

"He had to answer, he had to say something. So his answer was: 'Loyalty. Loyalty to Germany, loyalty to the party, loyalty to the Führer. How can a nation of eighty million people be wrong? Maybe I don't know all of the answers, but the Führer is great, and I must trust him. I have a duty to my country and my people. Therefore, I must do it. I must follow orders.'

"The Voice was there, he knew in his heart that this was a heinous, barbaric, and evil crime against humanity. In his heart he knew this, and he couldn't live with that. No human being could. And so he had to make a choice: either don't do it, or find some way of justifying it. Find some way that makes it better, that excuses it, that at least explains away the awful feeling of guilt that rests inside his human heart.

"So the Nazis did just that: they either made the choice that so few made — to resist and fight against the very culture they had been raised in, or they bought into the Nazi party lines. They swallowed the trash the ministry of propaganda was serving that day, and assuaged their conscience with bunk.

"Whatever opinion we have of those people, we must always remember that they were humans. If we label them inhuman monsters, we actually remove a level of culpability from them. They were human, and that is what makes them responsible for what they did. Every last one of them was guilty of the most horrific crimes imaginable. But to allow them to do this, there had to be a system that allows a human being, the height of creation, to willingly, knowingly commit demonic acts that we don't have words to describe. For this to happen, there had to be built into mankind this ability to believe whatever he wants to believe, whether it makes sense or not.

"I don't think that in the course of history you will ever find a man who set out to be evil. I don't think the human being ever existed who said, "I am evil, and wish to perpetrate only horrendous deeds.' Quite the opposite — everyone, no matter how depraved, no matter how far down the ladder of morality he has sunk, feels that what he is doing is right, that what he is doing is good. It has to be that way because of the very manner in which Hashem created man — man cannot do 'bad.'

"So where does that leave us? If every path that I set out upon will become good in my mind, regardless of whether it is or isn't — if every choice that I make ends up, in my mind, being proper because I have this inborn capacity to make everything right — how does a human truly know if his or her choices are moral and correct? And even more — how am I to find my path in this maze that we call life?

"To help us succeed, Hashem gave us the Torah, the only universal set of standards against which we can measure ourselves. Torah standards don't change with the times and aren't subject to interpretation based on our whims or moods. They are standards that stand the test of time because they were written to be eternal. They are standards that aren't prey to the passing winds of social reform, which views today's ideas as progressive and by tomorrow disparages them as antiquated.

"Since the Torah was written by our Creator, it is made up of universal codes, fundamental truths, and immutable laws that guide us through the tempest of uncertain social change. These allow us to successfully chart our course in life, whatever winds are blowing in the social air of our times. They allow us to see through the darkness of this world and reach truths — real truths, hard-core truths — that endure through the ages, helping us see past our own biases and desires.

"Torah is the program that allows the part of us that fundamentally understands and only wants to do what is right in life, to surface and gain primacy. Following the ways of the Torah brings a person to the heights of perfection. It is the one prescription that Hashem wrote so that man has a chance to perfect himself. It is the one formula for man's success, to bring forth all that is great in man, allowing him to reach that potential for which he was put on this planet. We only need to reach out for the Torah and study its ways."

"Rabbi," David said, and sighed, "that sounds much easier said than done."

Chapter Twenty-One

I'LL NEVER DIE

I won't grow up, I won't grow up,
I don't want to wear a tie, I don't want to wear a tie.
And a serious expression, and a serious expression
In the middle of July, in the middle of July...
I won't grow up, I won't grow up...not I.

(*Peter Pan*)

"David, do you remember the famous song from *Peter Pan*, 'I Won't Grow Up'?"

"Rabbi, I have to admit that it's been a while."

"If Lisa were here, she might recall it, but I understand her not being available. No matter. I find one point of particular interest in those lyrics — "I won't grow up, not I." I find it telling because this is how the immature mind thinks. 'The way things are now are the way they will always be.' Even if you confront an immature

162

person with the facts, and he fully accepts that things will *not* always be the same, he simply doesn't apply what you say to his everyday life.

"Picture this: It's a beautiful spring day, and little Tommy, a second-grader, doesn't want to go to school; he'd rather stay home and play. Here's what the conversation might sound like:

> **Son**: *"Mommy, I don't want to go to school."*
>
> **Mother**: *"Tommy, you have to go to school! If you don't, then when you grow up you won't be able to get a good job, and then you won't have enough money to buy a house and food and all the other things that you'll need. So I want you to be a good boy, get your jacket on, and get ready for the school bus."*
>
> **Son**: *"Oh, Mommy, I never thought of it in those terms! You are so right! I must get good grades so I can get into a good college, and then get into the master's program that I'm interested in, so I'll earn enough money to buy a nice home in the suburbs. Thanks for reminding me, Mommy. I'll get my coat on right now."*

"David, both you and I know this is *not* how the conversation would go. In fact, in our little scenario, Mother couldn't be more off the mark. Firstly, little Tommy has no real plans of ever being an adult. In his mental reality, he will always be a little boy, and his Mommy and Daddy will always take care of him. And, secondly, even if Tommy had the understanding that one day he *will* grow up, there is no way that he has the emotional maturity to begin the process of building credentials for something that is over twenty years into the future. But this point doesn't matter anyway because at his stage of development Tommy is certain that 'Mommy and Daddy will always be there to take care of me.'

"Signs of maturity are demonstrated by two criteria:

1. Emotional fortitude, which allows me to push off immediate gratification for a later benefit
2. The ability to see the big picture

"It's a long-held, accepted point of view that children aren't simply adults in small bodies. Their entire emotional system is unlike that of an adult's, and the major difference between them is the child's inability to envision the future, to be able to plan for events that are far off, or to envision the consequences of their actions — today, tomorrow, next week, or next month. Being able to clearly think about and plan for next year, five years from now, and even ten years down the road takes a considerable level of maturity. To a child, nothing is more valuable than 'right now.'

"Ask a five-year-old, 'Son, would you rather have a thousand dollars in two years or this toy fire truck?' and it's not even a contest! To him, some future crumpled pieces of paper don't hold a candle to that shiny red fire truck with working sirens and whistles.

"Many a well-meaning grandparent has been greatly disappointed at their grandchild's huge lack of enthusiasm and gratitude when the child realized that for Chanukah the *zeidy* had bought the child a modest mutual fund. The child couldn't care less for such a gift because at that age the future is something totally off the radar, and if it's not tangible and exciting, it's of no interest. Children live for the here and now. Their mood swings are huge because right now the greatest thing in the world just happened, so they are ecstatic, and ten minutes later, when they find out they are not going out for pizza as promised, you'd think their world just imploded.

"As children mature, they are able to better envision the future, to see themselves in other settings, to see themselves in different roles, and most significantly, to finally understand the concept of the word 'future.' They finally understand that one day they will need to support a family, raise children, and do their share for the community. That sense of seeing the future as if it were here now, of feeling emotionally that it really is going to happen, is a function of maturity.

"This concept of maturity, and its resulting widening of one's point of view to include the future, doesn't dependent on how smart or educated a person is. A person can have a very high IQ and be able to perform brilliant mental feats, yet have the maturity of a twelve-year-old. Even when we find the occasional child prodigy whose mental faculties are on the level of a twenty-year-old, her temperament is still that of her chronological age, and she might very well still behave like a child. Maturation is a process that often comes with age. Like a wine that ferments, with age the human mind is usually able to acquire a more mature, broader view of life.

"The wisdom to see the final results of my actions, the wisdom to see how this course of study will enhance my life, usually goes hand-in-hand with maturity. In fact, to many of the classic Jewish thinkers, one of the measures of wisdom is how far a person is able to envision the results of his or her actions.

"When Rabbi Chaim Brisker died, his son — Rabbi Yitzchak Zev HaLevi Soloveitchik (the Brisker Rav) — said: 'The world doesn't know what it has lost! My father could see fifty years into the future. And I can see clearly, but only the present...'

"To me, one of the most important manifestations of maturity and being able to understand what the future holds is our attitude toward dying — not to death in general, but toward my own death.

"David, let me ask you a question. Do *you* plan on dying?"

"I can't say that I spend a lot of time thinking about it, Rabbi, except during our sessions," David quipped. "But I am certainly aware that I'm human, and that my time will eventually come. All the same, I plan on being here for a good long time."

"David, you are not the only one who thinks like that. Let me share a story with you," I said. "My mother-in-law was in the kitchen one hectic Friday afternoon — cooking, cleaning, preparing for Shabbos. The phone rang; it was a telemarketer selling, of all things, gravestones. He started his pitch.

"'Ma'am, we offer the finest gravestones, made from imported marble, guaranteed not to chip, fade, or—'

"My mother-in-law answered in a low, calm voice, 'I don't need one, thank you, as I don't plan on dying.'

"'Madam, I don't mean to be morbid, but we all must go one day,' he responded.

"'I understand, sir, but I really don't intend to die.'

"'Madam,' he insisted, 'surely you know that your time, too, shall come.'

"'I guess you didn't hear what I said, sir. I have no intention of dying. But thank you for calling,' and with that she hung up.

"While my mother-in-law uttered her lines in jest, there was a lot of truth in what she said. None of us intend to die. We certainly are aware that it will happen, but it certainly isn't on our so-called front burner. Intellectually we know that we will die, but emotionally it remains in some far-off place, and we certainly don't live our life as if it will ever end.

"As a rule, mature people are responsible. They set aside money for retirement. They buy life insurance — just in case. They set up annuities for the grandchildren — who aren't even born yet. Everything in life is planned for. Everything is arranged. Yet, somehow, there is one detail that gets overlooked: what happens after they die?

"If dying were a serious possibility, wouldn't you spend time thinking about it? You planned your career. You carefully picked a neighborhood for your family to live in. You were highly selective in choosing schools for your children. When you were sick, you didn't say, 'We'll just wait and see what happens.' Every part of life was worked out — no stone was left unturned. It's only this one little area you forgot to deal with: the purpose of life and what happens to *me* when it's over.

"The reason we don't think about this fundamental topic is that we don't admit to ourselves that one day we will actually die. Of course, on one level we know it. I may be able to quote the annual death rate of people in my age bracket by region, but that remains a realization of the inevitability of death *in theory*. In the emotional realm, in my real mode of functioning, I don't face the fact that it will ever happen to me. So we go on living our lives without a care in the world.

The Chafetz Chaim explains that most of us believe there is a society of people who die — made up of older people, sick people, unlucky people. We believe that those unfortunates belong to this select group who die — and I? I am not a member. So while I may be very aware of death, it somehow doesn't apply to me.

"Amazingly, this is true in all times and is the mindset of all individuals — old and young, healthy and sick. I saw a telling example of this once when visiting my grandmother. In her later years, she would spend her summers in a hotel in New York's Catskill Mountains. I would visit regularly, and on one occasion we were sitting together with a number of her friends — all senior citizens. The conversation was pleasant until someone mentioned that 'so-and-so' had passed away. Another person commented, 'Oy! What a shame. All of the old people are dying!'

"I looked around at the group and was taken aback: not one person there was under eighty. They were all grandmothers and great-grandmothers. They had all lost their parents. Most had lost siblings; many had lost a spouse. Yet, to each of them, dying was still a distant concept. It wasn't real. On some level they believed that it was something that wasn't going to happen to them. It was *the old people* who were dying, the *unfortunate people,* a select group — and not one of them was a member of the Chafetz Chaim's 'society of those who die.'

"Taking this discussion one step further: If we really do understand that one day we'll die, I would think we'd spend some serious time thinking about this subject. But somehow that doesn't happen. Why?

"The answer is simple. We have this amazing capacity to totally block out this reality from our emotional operating mode. It's as if we are simply not equipped to deal with this reality. 'What do you mean I won't be here anymore, that I won't exist? I have always existed. I have been on this planet my entire life. Where else will I be but here?' Intellectually, logically, based on what we've seen since the world was created, we understand that life as we know it will end one day. We can discuss this concept, it makes sense to us, and we accept it. But on an emotional level we simply can't relate to it really happening to us.

"There is a deep-rooted reason for this phenomenon. When we spoke about Hashem creating man in a manner that allows for Free Will, we made the observation that the only way to make sure this happens was to keep an even playing field, where it is as easy to do bad as to do good. We also discussed that since man was created with a spiritual soul that is stronger than his animal soul, Hashem balanced the playing field by gifting mankind with the power of imagination. Now that he can 'believe what he wants to believe,' he has true Free Will to choose and to develop himself in a way that will lead to eternal reward. To maintain this balance, a fourth element had to be added to the human character: the inability to realize that one day we will actually die. If I were totally logical about life and saw an end to my days — not in a theoretical, intellectual manner, but for real, if I could vividly and graphically see that my tenure on this planet will come to an end and that my current state of existence will cease, that understanding would skew the entire process of living so that the playing field would no longer be balanced.

"I would be *forced* to deal with issues that would radically change the way that I approach life. I would be *forced* to confront this most vital of issues: What am I doing here? What is my goal? How can I best achieve that goal? If I could emotionally accept the fact that my time on Earth is limited, how could I possibly live my life pursuing frivolous goals? That reality alone would force me to ask: Why am I here? What is my purpose? How can I make every minute count?

"Don't you see, David? Because we can't emotionally accept that with each tick of the clock we are drawing a minute closer to leaving this life, we live our lives with little forethought, little attention to what's important, and little concentration on how we are spending our days. We simply follow the track that was set for us many years ago, hoping, praying, that it is the right path. But do we know for sure that how we conduct ourselves now is the best way for us to earn eternal bliss? Of course not. Why? Because mostly we just go from day to day like a drunk in his stupor, without a care in the world, and pay little attention to one detail, one issue — the purpose of it all — which is something most of us are simply too busy to deal with.

"You see, if we were to come face-to-face with the issue of eventual death, if we would ever be gut-wrenchingly, brutally honest with ourselves and ask, 'What is the purpose of it all?' then we would discover a very different perspective on life. It we were forced to confront this issue as if it was really going to happen to me — as if I will one day really leave this earth — that awareness alone would change the whole focus of our lives. My spiritual soul would demand, 'Do something! Contribute, accomplish. You only have a short while here. Discover your purpose, and pursue it for all you are worth.'

"If I was totally alert and existed with full emotional clarity — and understood that every action I take in my life shapes the person I will be for eternity — if I truly believed that when I die I will leave my current state and live on forever on the level of the person I was when I died — then of course that understanding would vastly change my current life. To do something improper would be like putting my hand in a fire, something that in theory I have Free Will to do but never would.

"The crystal-clear realization that this world is indeed an anteroom to the next would change my life to such an extent that I would no longer have Free Will, because that realization would not allow me to choose between right and wrong — I simply could not live on anything but the highest spiritual level. Gone would be any credit I could earn for overcoming temptation, gone would be further reward in the World to Come for contending with huge challenges, and prevailing.

"To retain my ability to earn a larger portion of reward after I leave this world, I must struggle mightily, and that can only be done when thoughts of what happens after we die are simply not on my agenda.

"And because this is so, it is extremely difficult for us to find our path in life. That is the battle for which we were placed on this planet. That is the struggle that we are given credit for winning. If the path was clear, if the way was easy to find, then our life would be that of an automaton, a creature preprogrammed to do only good. Our Free Will would be gone, and life on this planet would truly have no meaning.

"To avoid that tragedy, Hashem created us in this state of semi-maturity, in which certain thoughts and recognitions elude us. Most of all, the recognition that my life, as I live it, will come to an end is almost beyond my scope of thought.

"To me, one of the clearest examples of this phenomenon is teenage smoking. Smoking is a habit that millions of Americans wish they had never begun. I don't think you will ever meet a smoker who says, 'I'm *so* glad that I began this slow-death process that ruins my health, makes me feel sick, and is really annoying to everyone around me.' Most people actually curse the day they began. Yet I am constantly amazed as I pass the local public high school and see groups of teenagers — boys and girls — with cigarettes dangling from their lips.

"I live in a nice suburb; those kids in the schoolyard all come from good families. These are bright, nice kids who have received a stellar education in a drug-free environment, and yet there they are smoking. Why? Don't they understand that it's a self-destructive habit? Don't they know that they are damaging themselves every time they inhale? Why do they do it?

"Common wisdom tells us, 'It's peer pressure, they want to seem grown up.' 'It's rebelliousness, part of how they find themselves, how they assert their independence.' But I want you to think about this: Would a sane, rational person do something to damage themselves simply because of peer pressure? Would these same teenagers take a knife and cut off a limb? They wouldn't. I know many of them — they are intelligent, sensitive young people who can quote for you the exact statistical percentages of deaths in their age bracket from tobacco-related diseases. Yet they smoke.

"What is actually going on in their teenage minds is that they don't *emotionally* accept that this activity will lead to their early, painful demise. While they might spout to you all kinds of facts about the higher rate of emphysema among smokers, the increased chances of heart attack, the greater occurrence of lung cancer, they don't believe it will happen *to them*. 'I'll quit before it gets bad.' 'I have plenty of time before I'm old enough to get sick from this.' 'Don't worry about me; I can take care of myself.'

"But a more accurate description of what they're thinking is the message from the words in Peter Pan's song: 'I'll never grow up.' They are certain that old age won't happen to them. They feel immortal, invincible. No sane teenager would ever mouth those lines, because in our conscious mind we all know them to be absurd. But there is more that shapes our behavior than a rational, sane mind.

"In a similar vein, even mature adults are unable to focus on death. The reason for this is much like the one that pervades the immature mind: we are incapable of staying focused on the really big picture. For that reason, there is a third term that we should use: 'super-mature.' To me that connotes someone who possesses complete balance, who is living in this world but is aware of the greater purpose it offers. He is able to see what he does on this earth as important, very important — but he sees it fitting into a grander scheme of things. He actually 'gets' the totality of the picture, not only in an intellectual sense, as some memorized fact, but as something that is real to him, something he feels, something that affects the way he acts, the way he thinks, the way he approaches all the elements of life. He lives with the knowledge that he is here on Earth for only a few short years, that he has a very real and important mission on Earth, and that when his time is up he will appear in the World to Come at the exact level of spiritual achievement that he reached while alive.

"This emotional perspective changes every element of his life. Everything takes on a different, more significant meaning. This single mind shift changes his life as no other thought possibly could. Every minute of life becomes precious and meaningful. Even his suffering becomes significant, as it fits into a greater plan. He sees himself as a baby born in this world, he sees himself as he is now, and he sees himself after he has left this world. This super-mature vision is one of the most empowering abilities that a human can possess.

"But, David, I want you to understand that to move ourselves into the state of the super-mature, to have a true worldview of our life, isn't an easy goal to reach. As we discussed, this isn't an intellectual exercise. It isn't a question of acquiring some new information; it isn't an issue of our studying some texts, getting the correct life perspective, and then — whammo — everything changes. It is much more akin to a maturation process. We are dealing with a change in our emotional awareness. It is a growth process, one that take a lot of time, work, thinking — and constant reinforcement. Even after we have been exposed to this concept and are intellectually comfortable with our purpose in this world, we tend to lose sight of the bigger picture.

"Rabbi Yisrael Salanter, known as the father of the *mussar* movement, had a student who left Poland and moved to Paris. The word came back to Rabbi Salanter that his student, while quite successful in business, was neglecting his religious pursuits. Not long afterward, Rabbi Salanter had occasion to travel to France. When the former student heard about his mentor's arrival, he set out to meet him.

"At the train station, when Rabbi Salanter disembarked, the student stood anxiously waiting. He greeted his revered teacher, and after exchanging a few civilities, he asked, 'What brings the Rabbi to Paris?'

"Rabbi Salanter answered, 'I need a button sewn onto my coat.'

"The student was taken aback. *Surely the rabbi didn't hear my question*, he assumed. So he repeated, 'What brings the Rabbi to France?'

"Rabbi Salanter answered, 'I heard that there are some fine tailors in Paris, and as I said, I need a button sewn on my coat.'

"The student said, 'Surely there are enough experienced tailors back in Poland that the Rabbi didn't have to make such a long, difficult trip.'

"Rabbi Salanter responded, 'You can't believe that I would make such a long trip for something as inconsequential as sewing on a button? Yet your soul has made a much longer journey to come to this world, and you spend every waking hour indulging in trivial endeavors that do nothing to benefit your soul.'

"Let's put this into perspective. This student was a mature, successful individual. He had spent his youth growing in spirituality under the guidance of one of the greatest teachers of the generation. He didn't lack any intellectual understanding about the purpose of life. He had studied this subject, delved into it, spent many years involved in it, yet his life no longer reflected that understanding. It wasn't because of questions or doubts that he had, but simply because he got so caught up in the business of living that he lost focus on the reason behind it all.

"Rabbi Salanter was providing a wake-up call to remind his student of what he knew but was no longer a part of his operating mode. What he was saying was, 'I am not here to tell you anything new. These are points that you understand only too well. The problem is that you haven't taken the time of late to dwell on them, to ponder them, and to allow them to shape your behavior and life.'

"This is a very important message to us as well. If we would ever be gut-wrenchingly, brutally honest with ourselves and recognize that one day we will leave this earth, that awareness alone would change the entire balance of life. Our *neshamos* would scream out, 'Do something! You only have a short while on this planet. Discover your purpose and pursue it for all you're worth!' The result would be a life that is more directed, more passionate, and more meaningful. We would recognize the extraordinary value of life, and what we are here to accomplish. And we would be so much more alive — living by design, not by chance.

"The first step is to be aware of the importance of accepting the fact that we will eventually die. When we do, death becomes something that we embrace, and we find different venues and opportunities to experience it and make it real.

"You see, David, everything that we have been discussing until now is meaningless if it doesn't lead to action, if it doesn't cause you to change. If a person studies these concepts and says, 'Now I have an understanding about the true meaning and value of life,' but lives his life the same way he did up until that point, then clearly he didn't get the message. Because the message, while it may seem to focus on death, is actually about *life*. Not in the abstract, not in some philosophical discussion, but in a very real, concrete manner — focusing, altering, improving our day-to-day activities. The most powerful lesson that the inevitability of death has to offer us is one on how to live life.

"When a person has a near-death experience, life itself becomes so much more precious. When a young woman is diagnosed with late-stage cancer, every moment of her remaining life becomes charged with significance. Why? What changed? Only one key focal point: she now sees in a very real way that her life will, in fact, come to end. For the first time in her existence, she finally gets it. It finally, finally becomes real: she is going to die. And that focus changes everything.

"Why does living one's life meaningfully, in a way that will garner optimum eternal reward, have to wait until a person gets a tragic diagnosis? Why does it have to wait until it's too late to amass the eternal reward we all long for? If we allowed ourselves to focus on death, on *our* inevitable death, for just a short while — and in a way that led to a more meaningful life — then our lives would be so much more directed, so much more passionate, and yes, so much more meaningful. We would be able to live our life by design, not by chance, and we would be so much more alive."

"Actually, Rabbi, I feel very alive now. I mean, looking forward I see a great life ahead of me. And although I really appreciate all you've taught me, and I'm really happy I reconnected with you, well...I...don't know how to put this, but...would it really be that bad if I simply let things develop and see where it takes me?"

Chapter Twenty-Two

FRANK AND JOE

"David," I said, "I'd like to answer the question you left me with last week, because most people seem to have that attitude toward life: why not just go with the flow, as they say. But the truth is that we humans have a tendency to get so caught up in the details of life that we lose sight of where we are headed. Many times, we get into situations, and before we even realize what's happened to us, we are way down the garden path, down a path we never intended to be on. And then it's too late. We stand there wondering how this happened. *How did I get here? How did I ever get so caught up?* That is a reality of life. We become creatures of habit, and before we know it, we are in it deep, and we don't know how to get out.

"I recently read a post by a Jewish woman, who was grappling with the problem that her husband, who is Catholic, wants to bring a Christmas tree into their home. She couldn't quite identify why a tree in her house bothered her — but it did. It left her without peace. She discussed different solutions with her friends. Maybe putting a Jewish

Star on top. Only using blue and white decorations (the colors of the Israeli flag). Having Santa leave Chanukah *gelt* under the boughs as gifts. But, of course, none of them satisfied her ultimate confusion. And Chanukah, the holiday of light, brought her only darkness.

"What aggravates her dilemma tenfold is that her children are in the middle of this conflict. While her husband has agreed to bring them up as Jews, there is constant confusion. On Passover we eat matzah, on Yom Kippur we fast, on Christmas we gather around a tree. You could almost hear the desperation in her unspoken cry of 'How did I end up here?'

This is an intelligent, sensitive woman; she did not plan to get into this situation — it 'simply happened.' She met a nice guy, he was an honest, caring, and sensitive man, and they started bonding. A normal course of affairs. What she didn't realize back then was that she was making a decision. She was passively deciding to put herself into this situation — this situation that would result in her children's father being Catholic, and would put her in a dilemma that she can't resolve.

"In life, many of our crucial decisions happen that way. It is rare that we actually choose our path. We go about the business of living, and what happens...happens. We meet this person, get involved with this group, find ourselves spending time with these people, and life goes on. It usually isn't until years later that we wake up and find ourselves somewhere, wondering how we got there.

"If you speak to substance abusers, you will find that for many it begins as a simple kick. A friend turns them on to alcohol or drugs, and they find it has an appeal. It's fun. So they do it again. *Why not? Who's hurt? What's the damage?* And, theoretically, if a person didn't use drugs often and stopped when they were young, perhaps the damage wouldn't be that severe. But it never works out this way. The problem begins with that slow and insidious habit that begins forming. It starts to become that every time I come home from work, 'I need a drink.' Or every time something difficult happens in my life, 'I need to get high.' And it begins slowly at first, then little by little, until this person, a regular person, a person just like you or me, finds himself addicted — a slave to the bottle, or to pills, or to cocaine. And then he wonders: *How did I get here? How did it happen to me? How did I let myself get to this point?*

The answer is they never just got here. They never just found themselves at this point. It was a long and gradual road — it was a long slip down the slope, and the whole way down they never knew where they were headed. People don't decide to be a drug addict, or a wife beater, or a criminal, or any of the sociopaths that we read about in the papers. Life takes its course, and they proceed. It is only long after they are down that path, once it's too late, that they wake up and find out where they are.

"To show you what I mean, I would like to offer a parable.

"Frank and Joe go way back. They grew up as regular American guys. They were good friends in high school and then roommates in college. Since graduation they haven't seen each other, but Frank often finds himself thinking back to those good old days. Throughout their college years, Frank felt kind of bad for his friend Joe. Joe was a decent guy and all that, but when everyone else was out partying and having a good time, there was 'Joe the Geek,' studying. It seemed that Joe studied morning and night; you almost never saw the guy without a book in his hand. While everyone else was out there getting drunk, having a great time, there was Joe the Loser, sitting over the books. Poor guy.

"After graduation, Frank and Joe went their separate ways. Joe, the geek who ranked at the top in his class, went on to medical school and became a well-established surgeon. And Frank, well... Frank sort of drifted. He graduated college with straight Cs and never could find a job that he really liked. He ended up working behind the fish counter of a local supermarket.

"As fate would have it, the two meet many years later. Joe drives into the parking lot of the supermarket, parks his imported sports car, steps out and straightens his two-thousand-dollar, custom-made suit. As he walks into the store, who does he see working behind the fish counter? None other than his old friend Frank!

"'Frank, old buddy, how are you doing?'

"'Hey, Joe, is that you?'

"'Wow, Frank. It's been so long! How are you?'

"'Great, been a long time! Wow, Joe, you sure look different. Is that a custom-made suit? It looks great.'

"'Yeah, just got it. And Frank, you look, um, different... I really like your...oh, I mean your apron,' Joe responds.

"'Hey, Joe, what you driving these days?'

"'Well, I sort of just picked up this new Italian sports car... And you, Frank, what are you driving these days?'

"'Well, I'm driving this old hunker, just till I can afford something better.'

"'Listen, old buddy, really great seeing you.'

"'Yeah, you too, Joe. Maybe we'll get together to talk about old times.'

"'Sounds great, give me a call.'

"And then Frank starts thinking: *It sure does seem like my old buddy Joe has it made. He probably has lots of money, works four days a week, plays golf two afternoons a week, lives in a custom-built home, is happily married, and is active in his community. But more than that, he's doing something with his life, something important, something significant. And here I am, thirty-something, working behind a fish counter, making little more than minimum wage, driving a beat-up old jalopy, and living in a one-bedroom apartment. Going nowhere.*

"At that moment, it hits him. *How could I possibly have been so stupid? What an opportunity I wasted! All those years I used to look at Joe as a loser, and now look at him, and look at me.*

"And it isn't just at this moment that Frank will bemoan his fate. For the rest of his life, every time he scrambles to pay the rent, every time one of his kids says to him, 'Dad, how come so-and-so gets to go on vacation with his family and we never go anywhere?' he'll think about Joe. Every time Frank wakes up in the middle of the night wondering why he's caught in a dead-end job, going nowhere and doing nothing — just wasting away — he'll think about Joe.

"For the rest of his life, Frank will kick himself, and it will always come back to this one realization: *I blew it. I had the same chance Joe had. I could have made myself into something, and I didn't. I could really have been someone, and now look at me. Why? Not for any good reason. I just got caught up in all of the stupid things going on around me and lost focus on why I was in school in the first place.*

"Over and over again, the same haunting lyric will play in Frank's mind: *If only I could go back in time and do it over again.*

"But he can't. He had his shot. He had his one go-around, and he blew it. Now, for the rest of his life, he will remain what he made of himself.

"That moment is the most painful in a person's life. Because at that moment, the truth comes crashing through — you understand what you were capable of doing. You see the purpose of life and recognize what you could have achieved in your stay on this planet. In one flash of recognition, you perceive the greatness of man and what you were capable of accomplishing.

"And it is at that moment that you want to scream out: 'Please! Please! Please! Just give me one more chance. Just one more opportunity to spend some time working on myself, improving, changing myself. Please!' But it is too late. Life is over. This one chance at change, this one opportunity to grow, is gone. How you are at that moment in time is how you will be for eternity. And the realization that you could have been so much greater, and accomplished so much more, is the most tragic, heartrending moment in a person's existence.

"The beauty of being alive is that it is never too late. As long as there is breath in your lungs and blood coursing through your veins, you can change and grow. The real value of life is the difference that you can make for eternity. In yourself. In who you will be forever. That is why Hashem put us on this planet, and it is the only thing truly worth striving for.

"David, did you feel the power of the 'Frank and Joe' parable? Can you see how real it is, how similar to the lives we live? Mostly, we wake up too late to recognize the importance of life and the literally once-in-a-lifetime opportunity it gives us to perfect ourselves. Mostly, we get caught up in things, and before we know it, it's ten years later, twenty years later, and we don't even have a clue how we got where we are.

"But that only happens if we try to figure it all out on our own. Thank God, we don't have to do so. Hashem gave us a Torah, the one tried-and-true roadmap that guides us on how to enjoy our stay in this world while we accomplish the task for which we were placed here. The Torah, the Divine directive, shows us how to chart our course, and warns us repeatedly to keep mindful of what's important in life. And it admonishes us to keep studying it — to always review it and make Torah study part of every day of our life — because even when we are on the right path, since we are human we often lose sight of our ultimate goal. So we need to continually study Torah, come to deeper understandings, and keep focused — so that we don't lose sight of why Hashem created us.

"It's true that the Torah contains all kinds of rules — rules for conduct, rules for living our lives — and by nature we hate rules. We yearn for freedom; we wish to be unshackled, not to have to follow any set patterns or commands. If I recall correctly, David, this concern — your resistance to obligating yourself to a lifetime of following rules — is what brought you to my office. And from the few times Lisa joined us, although you told me that she is much more committed to living a Torah-true life, it appeared to me that she, too, isn't all that excited about living by the Book.

"But the Torah's rules are standards that not only allow us to reach our potential, they also enhance our stay in this world. The ways of the Torah are pleasant. They make our lives here on this earth better, not worse. Not only in the sense that they allow us to live a satisfying life but because they were designed by our Creator who only desires our benefit and wants us to enjoy every facet of life. Just as God's creation was custom-designed for our benefit and enjoyment, so too did He give us a system that will not only enhance our relatively short stay in this world but will also benefit us for eternity. Our job is to study that guide — that God-written and God-given Torah — make it part of our life, and bring our life up to the standards described in it.

"David, I trust you to convey to Lisa all of the concepts she missed hearing about, and I wish both of you a lifetime of joy and commitment. And I thank you sincerely for agreeing to come for one last session next week. Trust me, you'll hear things you never knew!"

Chapter Twenty-Three

THE ETERNAL PEOPLE

"David, I've introduced you to the writings of many rabbinical figures during our talks, so most of the people I'll be telling you about today might surprise you, but if you bear with me, I think this final meeting will put everything we've discussed into perspective.

"Adolph Hitler began his rise to power speaking in the beer halls of Munich. It was the early 1920s, in post-First World War Germany, and a few hundred party members would gather to hear his plans to restore the honor of the German Fatherland. The story is told that at one such meeting, amid the haze of cigarette smoke and the smell of Bavarian beer, Hitler's voice could be heard ranting about Germany's problems.

"'The misfortune of Germany is the Jews! The Jews are the reason we lost the war! The salvation of the German Fatherland rests on ridding ourselves of the Jews!'

"On and on he shrieked. Toward the back of the room sat an old man with a white beard — obviously Jewish — listening. When Hitler finally finished this hour-long tirade, the audience leapt to its feet in adoring applause. The old man also stood up and clapped. Long after the rest of the audience finished applauding and began shuffling out, the old man continued his ovation.

"Hitler made his way over to the elderly gentleman and screamed, 'Don't you believe that I am serious when I say the Jews are Germany's misfortune?! Don't you believe me when I say that I intend to rid Germany of the Jews?!'

"The old man, undaunted, turned toward Hitler and said, 'I assume that you meant every word of what you said. You must remember, though, that we are an ancient people and you aren't the first to hate us. Many years ago, the evil King Pharaoh of Egypt also hated us. He enslaved our people for over two hundred years. But God saved us from him, and in honor of that event we have the beautiful holiday of Passover, when the entire family gets together and celebrates. What a joyous occasion!

"'Many centuries later, a wicked man named Haman came to power. He also hated us, and was determined to annihilate us. God saved us from him too, and in honor of that experience we now celebrate the festival of Purim, a wonderful feast day, with joyous singing and lively dancing. Then came the Assyrian-Greeks, who attempted to assimilate us and who extinguished the sacred light of our Temple's Menorah. Today, we have an eight-day holiday called Chanukah, a festival marking our victory over that enemy. You, Hitler, hate us more than any of our previous enemies, so I couldn't stop applauding, because I am sure that when God saves us from you, we will rejoice more than at any other time!'

"There is no holiday that marks Hashem's saving us from the Holocaust. There is no day of celebration. There are no family gatherings, there are no traditions reminding us of the salvation.

"However, after all we suffered during the Holocaust, even after losing six million Jews, we are still here. Despite the Nazi regime's all-out effort to systematically annihilate our nation, we are still here to talk about it.

"You and I are still sitting here, discussing our heritage, contemplating its meaning, very concerned with passing down our traditions to the next generation so we can continue the chain that spans millennia — one generation passing down our traditions to the next one.

"The reality is that we are an ancient people. We have lived through centuries of exiles, suffering the greatest tortures known to mankind. From the destruction of the Second Temple almost two thousand years ago, we have lived through the Crusades, the Spanish Inquisition, blood libels, pogroms, persecutions, mass murders, and gassings.

"If man ever devised a method by which he could torture his fellow man, it was used against the Jews. If there was ever a diabolical means used by man to kill his fellow man, it was used on the Jews. We were stabbed, shot, hung, executed, starved, clubbed, burned, beaten to death, gassed, and cremated.

"And yet we are still here today. We are still around to tell the tale, as vibrant and as strong as ever. And one of the ultimate ironies that history has to offer is that century after century, after so many repeated attempts to slaughter, to destroy, to wipe out the Jews as a people, this nation still exists.

"But from a historical vantage point there is a rather ironic question that begs to be answered: where are our enemies? Where is the Egyptian empire? Where are the Romans, the Persians, the Babylonians? All those great empires have risen and disappeared. Where are their people now?

"Of all the ancient peoples who delighted in inflicting us with death and exile, we alone are here to talk about it. Of all the ancient people, the only nation that remains intact, unchanged, still alive and thriving, is the Jewish nation. The others enjoyed their moment of power; for a period of time their stars shone brightly, but then faded. During their era of power and glory they attempted to crush us, they attempted to vanquish the Jews, but they failed, and then they faded from the face of history, never to be heard from again.

"This is a very important concept for us to stop and think about, David. Sometimes it is difficult for us to see the hand of Hashem. We want to believe, we want to strengthen our belief in our Creator, but it's difficult. And people often cry out, 'If only I could witness at least one miracle, if only God would show me one sign of His power, of His love for His nation, it would strengthen my belief.'

"I say that if you want to see the hand of God, if you want to strengthen your belief in God, you need look no further than at the fact that we survived our two thousand years in exile. If you want proof that the Creator of the world orchestrates the events of history, if you want to see God controlling the minds of renowned statesmen, generals, and kings — you need look no further than our amazing history.

"The fact that the Jews are still around, despite the absurd odds against us, the fact that in every generation the leaders of nations have stood up against us to annihilate us and yet we are still here while they aren't is one of the strongest proofs of Hashem's power, and more significantly, of His running this world.

"Watch as He shepherds his people from exile to exile; watch as he leads them from land to land, allowing them to be expelled but never totally destroyed.

"David, you might think that I am biased because of my religious leanings, that I only view history this way because I am a rabbi.

"To dispel this misconception, I'd like to share with you a number of quotes from historians, none of them with any religious biases. Let's look at the history of the Jewish nation through the eyes of a secular historian.

"Let me read you an extract from *The Jewish Dispersion* by Jacob Lestschinsky:

> For 1,900 years from the destruction of the Second Temple (70 CE) to the establishment of the modern State of Israel (1948), the Jewish people have wandered literally around the world. This wandering was usually precipitated by intolerable spiritual and/or physical persecution. The scope of the Jews' nineteen-hundred-year exile is reflected in the lands from which they were, expelled, en masse.

"And now he is going to list for us those countries from which we were expelled.

> For example, in the third century (CE) they were expelled from Carthage (North Africa), in the fifth century from Alexandria (Egypt), in the sixth from provinces in France, and in the seventh from the Visigoth empire. In the ninth century they were expelled from Italy, in the eleventh from Mayence (Germany), in the twelfth from France, the thirteenth from England, the fourteenth from France, Switzerland, Hungary, Germany, and in the fifteenth from Austria, Spain, Lithuania, Portugal, and Germany. In the sixteenth and seventeenth centuries Jewish populations were expelled from Bohemia, Austria, Papal States, the Netherlands, the Ukraine, Lithuania, and Oran (North Africa). In the eighteenth and nineteenth centuries they were expelled from Russia, Warsaw (Poland), and Galatz (Romania).
>
> In the twentieth century, all Jews living in Nazi-controlled lands were deported, [with most of them annihilated] and from 1948 to 1952 [due to intensive discrimination and the

threat of extinction] hundreds of thousands of Jews managed
to escape from the lands of Egypt, Lebanon, Syria, and Iraq.

"If you count all the nations from which we were expelled, you have almost the entire United Nations listed! In fact, if you get a chance to visit the United Nations building, make it a point to notice the countless flags waving in the wind, and try to find the few flags of countries that did not banish us!

"The only ones that haven't are because no Jews ever lived in that country, or the country didn't exist before Jews found a haven in Israel or in a few Western democracies. Yet, with all that said, have you ever met anyone from the Visigoth Empire? What about the Roman Empire, or for that matter, the Assyrian-Greek dynasty? They have come and gone, and we alone are still around to talk about it!

"I challenge you to find a people that was so disadvantaged, so discriminated against, so universally hated and oppressed. And yet of all of the ancient peoples, the only one left intact and unchanged is the Jews.

"Here is another example of a non-Jew's awe at our survival, this one written by Leo Tolstoy, entitled 'What Is the Jew?':

What is the Jew? This is not as strange a question as it would first appear to be. Come let us contemplate what kind of unique creature is this whom all the rulers and all the nations of the world have disgraced and crushed and expelled and destroyed; persecuted, burned, and drowned, and who despite their anger and their fury, continues to live and flourish.

What is this Jew, whom they have never succeeded in enticing with all the enticements in the world, whose oppressors and persecutors only suggested that he deny (and disown) his religion and cast aside the faithfulness of his ancestors?!

The Jew is the symbol of eternity.

He is the one whom they were never able to destroy, neither bloodbath nor afflictions, neither the fire nor the sword succeeded in annihilating him. He is the one who for so long has guarded the prophetic message and transmitted it to all mankind. A people such as this can never disappear. The Jew is eternal. He is the embodiment of eternity.

"These are not the words of the Talmud that I just quoted, and we aren't reading an article published by a Jewish thinker. These words were written by a man who viewed world history with the one criterion necessary to reach such an observation: an open mind. He studied the course of human events, and in an unbiased posture reached the understanding that this people has a unique destiny and has an eternal role in history.

"I want to share one final piece, which was written by a French author, Jon DeBileda, during the latter part of the nineteenth century:

In essence the Jewish people chuckle at all forms of anti-Semitism. Think all you want and you will not be able to find one form of brutality or strategy that has not been used in warfare against the Jewish people. I cannot be defeated, says Judaism. All that you attempt to do to me today has been attempted 3,200 years prior, in Egypt. Then tried the Babylonians and Persians.

Afterward tried the Romans and then others and others.

There is no question that the Jews will outlive us all.

This is an eternal people.

They cannot be defeated, understand this!

Every war with them is a vain waste of time and manpower.

Conversely, it is wise to sign a mutual covenant with them.
How trustworthy and profitable they are as allies!

Be their friends and they will pay you back in friendship
one-hundred fold. This is an exalted and chosen people!

"What strikes me as so compelling, David, is that these men
weren't out to prove the truth of Judaism — far from it! They
weren't looking to find some redeeming feature of Jewish suffering.
They were scholars! And their conclusion:

This is an exalted and chosen people!

"Isn't that what we have been taught in the Torah? Isn't that
the point the *Chumash* makes repeatedly? Yet somehow it sounds
more powerful when it comes from the pen of people outside of the
Jewish nation, coming from a purely objective viewpoint.

"Even if we look at the most recent tragedy that has befallen the
Jewish people, the Holocaust, we find that with all of its brutality
and barbarism it couldn't accomplish the ultimate goal of its per-
petrators: the Final Solution to the Jewish Problem. Much to their
eternal shame, we are still here!

"I want you to read Hitler's last words to you, David, his final
instructions and testament to his followers, one last impas-
sioned plea:

Above all I charge the leaders of the nation and those under
them to scrupulous observance of the laws of race, and to
the merciless opposition to the universal poisoner of all
peoples, international Jewry.

"Hitler's vision was to set up a system of government to forge
the way for generations to come. His Third Reich was to last at least
one thousand years. Where are they now? And we — the thought

of whom consumed him in his last hours — the sheep among the wolves, are still around telling the story.

"What does this mean? What lesson do we learn from this?

"I would like to read to you a quote, but this is from one of the greatest Talmudic scholars of the eighteenth century. He was a rabbi, teacher, and leader of his people, Rabbi Jonathan Eybeschutz. He writes:

> Will the atheist not be embarrassed when he reflects on Jewish history? We, an exiled people of scattered sheep from antiquity, after all that we have brutally endured after thousands of years. There is no nation or people pursued as we. Many and powerful are those who aspired to totally destroy us, but they never prevailed. How will the wise philosopher respond? Is this extraordinary phenomenon truly by chance?

"Rabbi Eybeschutz is saying that one must come to the understanding that there is direction behind the course of this nation. It isn't by chance. There is a controlling force.

"And, going even further, here is an observation by one of the leaders of German Jewry of the early twentieth century, Rabbi Dr. Isaac Breuer:

> The "People of the Book," among the nations, is the most fantastic miracle of all, and the history of this people is literally one of miracles. And one who sees this ancient people today, after thousands of years among the nations of the world, when he reads the Scripture [the Old Testament] and finds that they prophetically relate clearly and simply the ever-transpiring Jewish phenomenon, and does not fall on his face and exclaim, "God, the Lord of Israel, He is God," then no other miracle will help him. For, in truth, this

individual has no heart to understand, no eye to discern,
and no ear to hear.

"Rabbi Breuer is telling us to see the hand of Hashem. You don't need to see the splitting of the sea, you don't have to witness plagues being brought upon a pagan society. If we open our eyes to the events of our history, we have in front of us one of the greatest miracles that a person could ever want to see: that we, the Jewish nation, are still around to tell the tale. Still here, still alive, despite every attempt by every nation and power to destroy us and vanquish us, to finally eliminate us as a people.

"We are still here and our enemies aren't. That is a miracle, says Rabbi Breuer; that alone will cause a person to fall on his face and say, 'God, the Lord of Israel, He is God!'

"I think that everything we could possibly say about world history and the unique destiny of our nation pales in comparison to the miracle that we witnessed with our own eyes in the last fifty years: our people living in our own ancient homeland, the land of Israel.

"After an exile lasting almost two thousand years, not only have we survived as a people, we have reclaimed a land that we left thousands of years ago, a land that was barren and desolate for centuries. When Mark Twain visited the land at the end of the nineteenth century, he called it 'an austere, barren wasteland.'

"That's what it was till a mere sixty to seventy years ago. And now we are back, and the land is in bloom, sprouting forth with life. Name another place where this happened. You won't be able to find one...our story is completely unique and impossible to explain. Is there any thinking person who would call this anything short of miraculous?

"Maybe even more wondrous is the fact that we are still in that land some seventy years later. We weren't exactly welcomed back into our homeland. As soon as the State of Israel was declared, the

Arab nations declared war. To the American Jewish community, this meant disaster.

"My father was in America in 1948, and he told me that when they heard that the Arab nations were attacking the fledgling State of Israel en masse, common wisdom predicted that there would be another Holocaust.

"American Jews were steeling themselves for the inevitable destruction that was to come. There was no way that such a small nation, so ill-prepared for war, could possibly hold out against the entire Arab world.

"Paul Johnson wrote a fantastic book called *A History of the Jews*. It is truly worth reading, and in it he writes:

> On May 14, 1948, the state of Israel was declared. The next day, five mechanized armies attacked...sizably larger than the small band of Holocaust survivors defending Israel.
>
> The entire armament of the Israeli forces consisted of 17,600 rifles, 2,700 Sten guns, 1,000 machine guns, and 45,000 soldiers.

"Do you know that in 1948 the land ratio of Arab land to Jewish land was 640 to 1? For every acre of land that Jews had, the Arab Nations had 640. Even more significant was the imbalance in population. Fewer than 5 percent of Jews alive at the time lived in Israel. A total of 650,000 Jews were surrounded and attacked by nations populated by fifty million Arabs. We were outnumbered 75 to 1.

"But that is only part of the picture. Before the United Nations declared Israel an independent state, Palestine was ruled by the British. They had very strict rules against Jews owning guns, which means that there certainly was no Israeli army. There were no military drills, no armaments, none of the normal exercises of military units. The best that we had were some small groups gathering together in secret cells. And all of this continued until May 14, 1948, and then — on May 15, five Arab nations attacked our new country, one day after we were granted official statehood.

"You can't create an army, a navy, and an air force overnight. The entire Israeli Air Force consisted of a few Piper Cubs — rickety, little single-propeller flying go-carts that were originally loaded with grenades, and only later fitted for machine guns.

"The Arab nations had enough manpower and weapons to easily defeat Israel. Can a nation so outmanned, so outgunned, possibly survive more than a few days?

"According to any intelligent assessment of the situation, a massacre was imminent. The voice of logic cried out: how could such a small, unorganized, untrained band with almost no previous military experience possibly survive against the might of the Arab Nations?

"Please keep in mind that for decades the Arabs were constantly at war one with the other. They had plenty of practice at this thing called war. The Arab Legion was an elite, well-trained fighting force. Trained by the British, they were a formidable foe. We had no air force, no navy, no army.

"Many a war has been lost because the defending nation had to fight on more than one front. In 1948, Israel wasn't fighting on one front — there was no front — they were attacked from every side. They were completely surrounded and had to defend borders that didn't exist. Each attacking nation threw its full weight into the fray, coordinating their armies, mobilizing their tanks and heavy artillery, and sending their air force in for support. Israel galvanized for this one final massacre.

"After one month, the UN called for a cease-fire. With all of the Arab world's gathered might, they couldn't vanquish this little sliver of a country, and they asked that world body to sue for peace.

"I remember as a boy reading a book called *The Birth of the Israeli Air Force*. One story described the Jews still under British rule, who began to fly single-propeller airplanes, Piper Cubs, on reconnaissance missions for the Haganah. Once the State of Israel was declared and the Arabs proclaimed war, those 'toy' airplanes now became the Israeli Air Force. But their planes weren't fighter planes, they weren't equipped with guns or bomb racks. The pilot would load a box of grenades behind his seat, fly low, and drop them on the Egyptian troops. This worked well enough, until our boys ran out of grenades.

"The story, as told in the book, states that one of the pilots, who had nothing with which to fight the enemy, thought for a moment and then asked for a case of soda bottles. His fellow soldiers thought he had gone mad, but he insisted. So when he took off on his next mission, he had cases of soda bottles behind him. As he flew low over the Egyptian troops, he dropped one bottle, and it hit the ground with a loud crash. The Egyptian soldiers, seeing a plane overhead and hearing an explosion, assumed these were bombs, and...they ran for their lives!

"While this may be a charming story of clever ingenuity, in the real world you don't win wars with soda bottles! You can't wage a war without arms, without soldiers, without tanks, and without artillery.

"Here is another story to give you a sense of how Hashem was holding His right hand over us:

"Beit Eshel was a small kibbutz, two miles outside of Beer Sheva. When war was declared, the kibbutzniks knew that they — being in the south — would be the first site to be attacked, so they prepared for the onslaught. They didn't have to wait long. The Egyptians began with a heavy artillery barrage. The settlers hunkered down in bunkers. They waited for the artillery attack to end, and prepared themselves for the infantry assault that would surely follow. The Egyptian army attacked, charging forward with more than seven hundred men. The fighting was fierce on both sides, yet the kibbutzniks bravely fought them off. This entire garrison of trained professional soldiers failed to overtake the kibbutz.

"The truly amazing part was that the kibbutzniks were not trained soldiers, and at the time of the attack the complete arsenal of the kibbutz consisted of twelve rifles and two machine guns!

"In the real world, you can't fight off a garrison of soldiers with twelve rifles and two machine guns. Life just doesn't work that way. In the real world, people get killed, the stronger soldiers prevail, the better-armed troops win the war, and the better-trained military power is victorious — and there is no way that Israel should have remained on the face of the map.

"The story of Israel's War of Independence reads like a fable. If you study the events, you have to conclude that it couldn't really have happened that way. There must be some other explanation. But that is what happened — not long ago, but right in our day and age. No one expected the outcome as it happened. Certainly, the Arab nations didn't.

"Azzam Pasha, then the Secretary General of the Arab League, proclaimed over the airwaves: 'This will be a war of extermination, and a momentous massacre.'

"Over the next forty years, the Arab States spent more than three times the amount of money on military weapons than Israel did. Keep in mind that this was during the Cold War. Egypt and Syria had the backing of the USSR, not only in providing weapons, but in military training and strategy.

"Granted, eventually the US began providing aid to Israel, but the scope of supplies and training didn't compare to what the Soviets were giving to the Arab bloc. Between 1948 and 1973, a span of twenty-five years, the Arab nations declared war four times on this puny, understaffed country. Yet they could not boast even one victory. Try and try again, they just couldn't defeat Israel!

"Even now, when the land ratio is 250 to 1, they are so afraid of all-out war with Israel, they have resorted to acts of terrorism instead!

"To give you a sense of perspective, I would like to read to you an excerpt from a secular Israeli newspaper, *Maariv*. In an article that appeared on April 17, 1983, we read:

> *Is this how things really happened? Just as they are told in the history books? That 650,000 Jews who had escaped from the horrors of the Second World War, and from the cruel struggle with the oppressive British, did they really build up this whole infantry on their own efforts? Six-hundred-fifty thousand who created a nation-state from emptiness and desolation, and they stood in bitter warfare against the organized armies of five Arab countries?*
>
> *Only five percent of the Jewish people, and not only did they strike a blow against every enemy that stood up against them, but absorbed hundreds of thousands of refugees from the remnants of European and Middle East Jewry!*
>
> *By all logic and by all human reasoning, everything that happened in 1948 is in the category of the impossible. It was impossible, with the limited arms that the Jews possessed, with the rudimentary international support they managed to garner, with the limited resources that were available to them, to do all that they did. To bring a system of public services into operation from nothing. To establish a military from its beginning. To sustain supplies and minimal services, and to run a war that had no clear delineated front or rear lines, no organized lines of defense, no organized reserves of ammunition, and no expert commanders to lead its battalions!*

"Those are the words of a secular Israeli journalist, looking back on the events some thirty-five years later.

"Allow me to quote a story told by Rabbi Asher Wade. The story began on an army base in Berlin in 1974. Rabbi Wade, then a chaplain, befriended a Jewish American officer named Stuart. Stuart did not strike him as being a religious man, and so Rabbi Wade was surprised one day to see Stuart wearing a yarmulke (skullcap). Upon questioning Stuart's reasons for donning this unconventional attire, Stuart told Rabbi Wade this fascinating story.

> *As part of our first-year studies, cadets were enrolled in a course called "History of Military Tactics and Field Strategies," taught by a three-star lieutenant general with a PhD in military strategy. The course surveyed the major battles in history, including those of the Ptolemies, the Romans, the Middle Ages, and down to the latest battles of our modern era. During the final two weeks of the course, which were devoted to reviewing the material, I raised my hand with a question.*
>
> *"Why," I asked, "did we not survey any of the battles fought by the Jews, either of ancient times (i.e., Roman-Jewish wars) or of modern times (i.e., Arab-Israeli wars)?"*
>
> *The normally friendly general snapped back with an order for me to see him in his office after class. Upon entering the general's office, I was ordered to close and lock the door. The general then told me that he could only answer my question in the privacy of his office.*
>
> *"Do not think that the staff here at West Point has left the Jewish wars unnoticed," began the general. "We have examined and analyzed them and we do not teach them at West Point," he continued.*
>
> *"According to military strategy and textbook tactics, the Jews should have lost the wars. You should have been swept into the dustbin of history long ago. But you were*

not. You won those wars against all odds and against all military strategies and logic."

"This past year, we hired a new junior instructor. During a private staff meeting and discussion, the Arab-Israeli wars came under discussion. We puzzled at how you won those wars. Suddenly, this junior instructor chirped up and jokingly said, 'Honorable gentlemen, it seems to be quite obvious how they are winning their wars: God is winning their wars!' Nobody laughed. The reason is, Soldier, that it seems to be an unwritten rule around here at West Point that God is winning your wars, but God does not fit into military textbooks! You are dismissed," concluded the general.

I left the general's office. I had never been so humiliated in my life. I felt about two inches tall. "Wouldn't you know it," I said to myself, "that I would have to come to West Point and find out how great my God is from a nonpracticing Presbyterian three-star general."

I went back to my dorm room and dug down in my sock drawer to find that "flap of cloth" that I would throw on my head once a year. I said to myself, This thing is going on my head, because I had found out, in essence, who I was and where I came from.

"These words, that 'God is fighting your wars,' were said not by a Jew. They weren't uttered by a rabbi. They weren't a quote from the Talmud. They were spoken by a three-star Presbyterian general!

"David, I rest my case."

CONCLUSION

Behold days are coming, says God, and I will send a famine into the land, not a famine for bread, nor a thirst for water, but rather to hear the word of God.

(Amos 8)

We live in truly wondrous times, times where we enjoy unparalleled progress in many aspects of life — health, education for all segments of society, human rights, and comforts and conveniences that were unheard of even one generation ago. We enjoy freedom from oppression, and an openness and tolerance that allows mankind to flourish. Technological inventions and improvements are introduced at a dazzling pace, each one outdoing what was yesterday considered "state of the art."

We also live in a generation that hungers for meaning and purpose. We live in a generation that honestly yearns for spiritual fulfillment. We, the Jewish people, were gifted with the greatest, most fundamental system for spiritual enlightenment — the Torah — the guidebook written by God Himself. Torah is a beacon, a light tower to guide us through the turbulent sea of life so that our days are filled with purpose and pleasure as we journey toward our ultimate destination: eternal bliss in the World to Come. More than a book of knowledge that spices our sojourn on Earth, the Torah is the very essence of our life.

The Torah contains all of the wisdom of the universe, because the One Who created the cosmos wrote it to serve that purpose.

Our mission is to seek it out and quench our parched souls with its life-giving waters. If we haven't yet been fortunate enough to have had the opportunity to study Torah seriously, we owe it to ourselves to do so. Perhaps we were never exposed. Perhaps we were exposed but never took it seriously, allowing our fears to stop us from connecting. Whatever the case, let's seek out opportunities to learn and understand what we do — and why we're here.

The Torah's ways are pleasant, and so the journey — while taking commitment, courage, and fortitude — is inspiring and pleasurable. In all my years of teaching Torah, I have never met anyone who complained that its ways were harsh. The only issues have been: am I open enough to listen, and am I willing to invest the time and effort necessary to understand its approach?

Today, there is a great light that beckons. A generation of young men and women thirsting for a meaningful life and open to reconnecting to the golden chain of their families' pasts are demanding a way back. A young generation of teachers who speak the language of our newly seeking brethren are lighting up the pathways of return. Tens of thousands of young people who grew up with practice but little real knowledge are opening their minds and hearts to God and His Torah.

TWO WORLDS, ONE CHANCE

We were placed in this world with almost unlimited potential, and challenged to make ourselves great. We were given one shot at life. What we make of ourselves while we live is what we remain for eternity. The ways of the Torah are pleasant, so the passage, while requiring courage and fortitude, is enjoyable. When a person lives by the Torah's ways, he gains two worlds. By living a meaningful, fulfilling life he acquires this world and the World to Come. When he chooses otherwise, he loses both. Two worlds. One chance.

May you choose wisely, and may your journey be successful.

AFTERWORD

WHERE DO YOU GO FROM HERE?

I hope that you have found this book meaningful. While it offers information, its primary purpose is to impart a perspective — a perspective that should be the underpinnings of everything that you do. If this book brought you to think about the big issues of life, then I consider it a success — it has done its job. The question is: where do you go from here? How do you maintain that perspective? How do you apply it to your life? What is the next step?

Certainly, there is no one answer, as this is one of the great challenges of life. To deal with this issue, a wealth of material has been developed by Torah giants over hundreds of years. The difficult part is accessing that material. Many people find applying the *mussar* works a daunting task, one that just doesn't seem to work for them.

A tool that I would like to suggest is "The Shmuz." The Shmuz is exactly what the title implies, a *mussar* talk that deals with a wide range of subjects: davening, *emunah*, *bitachon*, marriage, parenting, people skills, working on anger, jealousy, and humility, and more. At this point, there are hundreds of lectures, and the list is growing. Similar in style to the book you have just read, the Shmuz takes Torah sources and applies them to life — to your life in the twenty-first century.

The lectures are available in a number of portals, and one is TheShmuz.com. There you can listen, watch, read, or download a podcast. I welcome you to look around the site. You will also find many other *shiurim* and materials there. There is also a Shmuz app for both iPhone and Android, which you can find by looking for "TheShmuz" on Google Play or the App Store.

If you try to avoid internet usage, you can listen to the Shmuz on Kol Halashon. Our direct line is 718-906-6461.

If you would like more information or would like to bring The Shmuz to your community, please call the Shmuz office at 1-866-613-TORAH (8672). I also welcome any thoughts or comments. You can reach me by e-mail at rebbe@theshmuz.com.

Following this page is a listing of the *shmuzin*.

LIST OF SHMUZIN

Eternal People

Rosh Hashanah:
Issues of the Day

Yom Kippur:
The Power of Teshuvah

Appreciating Olam Hazeh

Appreciating Our Wealth

It's Not Geneivah,
It's Shtick

Noach:
Understanding Belief

Power of Prayer

Akaidas Yitzchak

Questioning G-d:
Finding and Keeping
Your Bashert

Kibud Av of Eisav,
Appreciating Parents

People of Principle

Free Will, Part 1:
Nefesh HaBahami,
Nefesh HaSichli

Living Like a Rock

Chanukah:
G-d Fights Our Wars

Olam Haba: The Greatest Motivator

Acquiring Olam Haba the Easy Way (Everyone Needs a Mike)

The Difference between Emunah and Bitachon: Four Levels to Emunah

Free Will, Part 2: I Never Do Anything Wrong

Davening: Making It Real

Choosing a Career

Evolution: Does It Make Sense?

I will never die. Not me. No way.

Understanding Life Settings

They Don't Make Anti-Semites Like They Used To

Purim II: Don't Bite the Stick

Lashon Hara, Squandering Our Olam Haba

Respecting the Institution, America the Beautiful

People Believe What They Want to Believe

The Busy Generation

Anger Management

The Voice Inside

Understanding Nature, Putting the WOW Back into Nature

Where Was G-d During the Holocaust?

Israel: Exalted Nation / Oppressed People (Why Did G-d Allow the Holocaust to Happen?)

Hashem and Man: Master and Servant (Understanding Humility)

For the Love of Money

Three Types of Miracles: The Fifth Level of Emunah

Where Is Hashem: The Sixth Level of Emunah

I Need, Needs

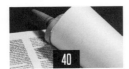

Acher, the Importance of Torah, Founding an Organization

Rebbe Akiva and Rochel, Potential of the Individual

Tricks of the Soton

Soton Out of the Box

Bar Kamtza: Do You Really Have Free Will?

WYSIWYG, Developing Willpower

Greatness of Man,
Beyond Our
Understanding

Cognitive Restructuring

Being a Nice Guy

Yom Kippur:
The Capacity of a Human

Bitachon, Part I:
Learning to Trust
Hashem

Bitachon, Part II

Bitachon, Part III

I Hate Criticism

Understanding Laziness

Staying Pure
in an Impure World

The Death of
Right and Wrong

Torah: Creating Worlds

Arrogance Misdirected

Humility:
An Issue of Perspective

Tidal Waves
and Middas HaDin

Heroes!

*Plan Your Life /
Live Your Plan*

Davening, Part I

Davening, Part II

*Davening, Part III:
Power Prayers, the
Impact of Tefilah*

Torah Mark of the Man

*Understanding and
Eliminating Jealousy*

People Skills

*Yitzias Mitzraim:
A War of Ideology*

*Onah:
The Torah's Sensitivity
to Another's Pain*

*Chesed:
Being Like Hashem*

*Respecting Others:
The Students
of Rebbe Akiva*

*Self-Respect:
The Basis of It All*

D'Vaykus in Our Times

The Art of Appreciation

**Asking Advice:
Second Torah Retreat**

Man-Based Morality

Kiddush Hashem

Reward and Punishment

It's Never Too Late

All for My People

**Why Me?
Understanding Suffering**

**The Moon Was Jealous,
Understanding
the Forces of Nature**

Why Me?

MOTIVATION!

To Tell the Truth

SELF-CONTROL

**Chanukah:
The Effect of Outside
Influences**

Malbin Pnei Chavero

Torah Lishmah

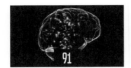

I Never Forget

Tact

*Shabbos —
Foundation of
Our Emunah*

On Being Judgmental

Time Management

*Purim III:
Seize the Moment*

Living the Good Life

*The Power of Positive
Thinking*

Men Are from Mars

Keeping the Dream Alive

Why Pray

Learning to Love Hashem

*Torah Study:
The Key to It All*

Parenting 101

*Understanding Life
Settings, Part II*

The Power of a Tzibbur

CHAZAK!

Servant of Hashem

MACHLOKES!
The Damage of Conflict

Becoming a
Great Individual

Sustaining
Spiritual Growth

Chesed:
The Essence of Judaism

Teshuvah:
Two Elements of Sin

Creating a Balanced
Self-Esteem

Preparing for Yom Kippur

GROWTH

OPTIMISM

Daas Torah

Bris Milah

Thrift

121

EMES: The Whole Truth

122

Parenting 102

123

Chanukah:
Whose Side Are You On?

124

Life Is Like a Box
of Chocolates

125

Business Ethics

126

Dignity of Man

127

Breaking the Forces
of Habits

128

Kiruv:
The Message
and the Medium

129

HaKaras HaTov:
Recognizing the Good

130

Living with Bitachon

131

Working for a Living

132

Purim: Being Human

133

ReJEWvenate

134

Parenting 103:
Setting Limits

135

Imagination:
The Devil's Playground

136

I'm Never Wrong

137

Being Sensitive

138

The Potential and the Present

139

The Power of Speech

140

The Arabs and the Jews

141

Parenting, Part IV: Sibling Rivalry

142

The Power of Laughter

143

Stages of Change, Part 1: Denial

144

Stages of Change, Part II: Support Groups

145

Stages of Change, Part III: Taking Action

146

The Impact of One Mitzvah

147

Finding G-d

148

Rich, Richer, Richest: How to Be Wealthy

149

The System of Teshuvah

150

Being a Religious Atheist

151

Be Brave, Be Bold

152

In G-d's Image

153

Marriage:
A Work in Progress

154

Marriage:
A Work in Progress,
Part II

155

Chanukah:
Flexi-dox Judaism

156

Get Out of Debt

157

Learning to Love
Learning

158

Me and My Big Mouth

159

212 Degrees,
Just One Degree Hotter

160

Purim:
Sheep to the Slaughter
and Concert Bans

161

April 15th:
The Test of Emunah

162

Learning to Care

163

Only the Good Die Young

164

I Hate Criticism:
The Mitzvah of Rebuke

165

The Art of Listening

Everybody Is Doing It!
The Effect of Society on Us

Sefiras Ha'Omer
Countdown to
Kabalas HaTorah

Emunah

Anger: Taming the
Monster Within

Sweet Revenge

Don't Sweat the
Small Stuff

Tisha B'Av 2,000 Years
Later, Where Are We?

Children of Hashem

The Illusion of Reality

Rosh Hashanah Prep,
Yom HaDin

Teshuvah Shmuz:
A Diamond with a Flaw

Being Grateful

To One Person You May
Be the Whole World

The Commitments
of a Jew

Why We Want
Moshiach Now

Emunah in Difficult Times

*Tolerating Evil:
A Perspective on
Recent Events*

*With Perfect Faith:
Bitachon in
Turbulent Times*

The Galus Mentality

Responsibility

G-d for the Perplexed

*Self-Mastery:
The Key to Good Middos*

*Rich Man, Poor Man:
The Ferris Wheel of Life*

Encounters with G-d

My Rebbe

*Combating Robotic
Judaism*

Hashem Really Cares

A Clash of Civilizations

*Tisha B'Av: What We Can
Do to Bring the Geulah*

Stop Playing G-d!

I'd Be the First to Thank Hashem If…

Teshuvah Shmuz: Limiting Beliefs

Life-Transforming Moments

Lashon Hara, Mindless Chatter

Chanukah: The Power Given to Man

Outcomes and Intentions

Disneyland USA, the ADD Generation

Listening to Your Messages

The Giant Within

Teshuvah Shmuz: A Fresh New Start

The Whatever Generation

Why Is Life Such a Battle

Putting G-d Back into the Religion

Putting Joy Back into LIfe

The Tiny Giant Called "I"

**Hashem Waits for
Our Teshuvah**

**Fleeting Glimpses
of the Upper Worlds**

Love the Life You Live

**The Incredibe Power
of Prayer**

Understanding Suffering

**Looking Back on a
Year Passed**

Difficult Life Situations

**Super Hurricanes
and Changing Realities**

Dealing with Failure

The Cause and the Reason

**Ahmadinejad,
the Palestinians,
and the Modern
Purim Story**

**Inside Out:
Heaven's System
of Judgment**

**Respect:
Can a Marriage
Survive Without It?**

**Marriage:
A Unit of One
and I'm the One**

**Marriage:
I Can't Respect Him/Her**

229

Communication in Marriage

230

Marriage: The Art of Apology

231

Women Are from Venus

232

Tisha B'Av: What We Lost

233

If We Knew What Our Prayers Do

234

Man Dependent on Hashem

235

One Small Step for a Man

236

How to Talk So That Hashem Listens

237

The Damage of Sin

238

Teshuvah Is Easy, It's Change That's Difficult

239

Being Wise to Yourself

240

The Gratitude Principle

241

The Gratitude Attitude

242

Marriage: Second Time Around

243

Needs of the Soul

Weapons of Mass Distraction

Appreciation: The Cornerstone of Emunah

Tisha B'Av: A World Unraveling

Teshuvah Shmuz: Maybe It's My Fault

Dealing with Tragedy

What Happened to My Bitachon

Moshiach: What's in It for Me?

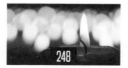

Kindliness Is G-dliness

If I Were a Rich Man

Learning to Love Hashem

Biases and Prejudice in the Courtroom of My Mind

Teshuvah Shmuz 5776: In the Days to Come

A Mitzvah to Listen to the Rabbis

Is It True Love: Dating Shmuz

Hashem Loves Me

259

What's Wrong with a Rainbow

260

Holy Pleasures

261

Tisha B'Av 5776: What Are You Waiting For?

262

Rosh Hashanah 5777: Being Mamlich Hashem

263

Yom Kippur 5777: Finding the Real You

264

Tishah B'Av 5777

265

Rosh Hashanah 5778: Knowing Hashem

266

Yom Kippur 5778: Appreciating and Achieving Greatness

267

We Only Fight with Friends

LIST OF SHMUZ SERIES
MAJOR SERIES:

Emunah in the Workplace: Earning, Spending and Saving from a Torah Perspective; introduction plus 8 full-length shiurim

The Fight: A Frank Strategy and Plan for Conquering Desire; introduction plus 12 full-length shiurim

Life 101: Explanations, understandings, and real-life examples based on the first perek of Mesillas Yesharim; 16 shiurim

The Bitachon Workshop; a series of 24 recorded shiurim outlining the basics of bitachon and emunah

The Marriage Seminar; a 12-session comprehensive guide to the Torah perspective on marriage

The Tefilah Project: Making Our Davening Understandable, Meaningful and Impactful; a 10-part series

The Tefilah Project 2: Making Our Davening More Understandable, Meaningful and Impactful; a 10-part series on Shemoneh Esrei

Humility, Arrogance & Self-Esteem: Becoming a Whole Person; a 6-part series

Guard Your Tongue: A Practical, Engaging Guide to the Laws of Shemiras Halashon (Speech); a 5-part series

The Pursuit of Happiness; a 9-part major series that will give you the tools, inspiration and system to acquire happiness

The Dating Seminar: Giving You the Clarity You Need in Shidduchim; 4 long shiurim and 12 short shiurim

Sefer Yonah: Pathways to Teshuvah; a 4-part CD series that allows you to gain clarity and understanding about Sefer Yonah

Purim: The Story Behind the Story: A Verse by Verse Analysis of the Megilah; a 4-part series

Pesach: Living Through the Makkos: A Verse by Verse Analysis of the Exodus; a 4-part series

Hilchos Teshuvah Boot Camp; a 3-part motivational, inspirational CD series that will both give you a better understanding of the teshuvah process and provide the drive to make these Yomim Noraim more meaningful

At The Foot of Har Sinai; a 4-part series that details and illuminates the experience of the Jewish People receiving the Torah, as explained by the Gemara, Medrash, Rishonim and Acharonim

ABOUT THE AUTHOR

Rabbi Ben Tzion Shafier is the founder and director of the famous www.TheShmuz.com, with hundreds of free *shmuzin* download-ed regularly by tens of thousands of men and women around the world. He is the author of the bestselling *Stop Surviving, Start Living; Finding and Keeping Your Soulmate; The Torah Lifestyle;* and *Two Minutes to Bitachon*. "The Shmuz" itself is a forty-five-minute weekly *shiur* that has been loved around the globe for over ten years. Rabbi Shafier's cutting-edge Torah content is available through live webinars, videos, articles, and more.

Rabbi Shafier lives in Monsey, New York, with his wife and family.

ABOUT MOSAICA PRESS

Mosaica Press is an independent publisher of Jewish books. Our authors include some of the most profound, interesting, and entertaining thinkers and writers in the Jewish community today. Our books are available around the world. Please visit us at www.mosaicapress.com or contact us at info@mosaicapress.com. We will be glad to hear from you.

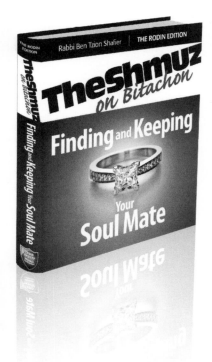